DATE DUE			
DEC 19 2002			

SWITZERLAND

MODERN
NATIONS
—OF THE—
WORLD

TITLES IN THE MODERN NATIONS OF THE WORLD SERIES INCLUDE:

Austria
Brazil
Canada
China
Cuba
England
Ethiopia
Germany
Greece
Haiti
India
Italy
Japan
Jordan
Kenya
Mexico
Norway
Russia
Saudi Arabia
Scotland
Somalia
South Africa
South Korea
Sweden
Switzerland
Taiwan
United States

SWITZERLAND

BY PATRICIA D. NETZLEY

LUCENT BOOKS
P.O. BOX 289011
SAN DIEGO, CA 92198-9011

Library of Congress Cataloging-in-Publication Data

Netzley, Patricia D.
  Switzerland / by Patricia D. Netzley.
      p.   cm. — (Modern nations of the world)
  Includes bibliographical references and index.
    ISBN 1-56006-821-3 (alk. paper)
    1. Switzerland—Juvenile literature.   [1. Switzerland.]
  I. Title. II. Series.
    DQ17 .N48 2001
    949.4—dc21

                                                                00-011485

Copyright © 2001 by Lucent Books, Inc.
P.O. Box 289011, San Diego, CA 92198-9011
Printed in the U.S.A.

CONTENTS

INTRODUCTION
A WEALTHY AND PRODUCTIVE NATION

Switzerland is a relatively small country, with an area of approximately 15,941 square miles, and most of its landscape is too mountainous to be inhabitable. Yet it has a fairly large population, with about 7 million people. What accounts for this level of growth is Switzerland's many natural resources, including numerous rivers and lakes, as well as its position at the forefront of business in many arenas.

The country is most famous for producing chocolate, pharmaceuticals, watches, clocks, and other precision instruments, textiles, and wine. It is also the destination of millions of tourists every year. They come to enjoy the many recreational opportunities offered by Switzerland's varied landscape, which ranges from pastoral valleys to glacial peaks. Tourists are also drawn to the mixture of old and new in Swiss cities. Many of these cities were founded in the Middle Ages, and they retain architectural features from that era.

Businesspeople, too, make Switzerland a prime destination. One reason for this is the country's numerous financial institutions. The Swiss have keen minds when it comes to investments; as the French philosopher Voltaire once said, "If you see a Swiss banker jump out of a window, follow him. There is surely money to be made."[1] The country has also produced a number of prominent intellectuals throughout history. There have been more Nobel Prize winners from Switzerland per capita than from any other country. Moreover, Switzerland has registered more patents for inventions than any other country.

The Swiss are known for their humanitarian efforts as well. The country supports a variety of organizations dedicated to promoting peace throughout the world. It also takes a neutral position in all foreign wars, meaning it refuses to take sides in any dispute. As a result of their peaceful nature, the Swiss cooperate well with one another, to the benefit of the entire country. Travel writer Mark Honan reports,

The Swiss have a way of making the unexpected work. Like successfully knitting together people from four language groups into one small nation. When travelling around the country, the visitor gets a flavour of Germany, France, and Italy, but always seasoned with a unique Swissness. The Swiss political system is one of the most complicated in the world, yet citizens dutifully inform themselves of the issues and vote regularly in a whole host of referenda. Every adult male has an army rifle at home but nobody goes around blowing people's heads off. British trains are late if a few leaves fall on the line in autumn, yet Swiss trains go over, round, and through the Alps [mountains] and still generally arrive minute-perfect. Things work in Switzerland—and work well.[2]

But Switzerland did not always work well. Until modern times, peace and prosperity were continually damaged or even destroyed by conflicts among various small groups of Swiss. As the Austrian chancellor Klemens von Metternich

The vineyards of Switzerland produce the wine for which the country is famous.

wrote in 1845, "The [Swiss] Confederation staggers from evils into upheavals and represents for itself and for its neighbours an inexhaustible spring of unrest and disturbance."[3]

The Swiss people were once extremely warlike, fighting not only with one another but also with numerous invaders from surrounding lands. Even after the invasions stopped, the Swiss continued to fight foreigners by hiring themselves out as soldiers in other countries' conflicts. Today, however, the Swiss are dedicated to ending wars throughout the world. This transition from war to peace, from disunity to unity, is one of the most interesting in the history of developing nations. Studying it leads to an understanding not only of Switzerland's past but also of its character as a modern nation.

A Divided Land

Today the Swiss are a unified people, but this was not always the case. The country's first settlers, who came from several different cultures, had trouble getting along and often fought over territory. Switzerland's geography contributed to this divisiveness. The landscape's numerous rivers, lakes, and mountains served as natural boundaries that cut groups of people off from one another. At the same time, the country's position within the heart of Europe, combined with its rich natural resources, continued to attract new settlers who did not fit in with existing tribes. They typically came from the lands ringing Switzerland's borders, now known as Germany, Italy, France, Austria, and Liechtenstein.

MOUNTAIN RANGES

People invading Switzerland from the south or southeast had to cross its most formidable natural boundary, a mountain range called the Alps. This range actually comprises two roughly parallel rows of mountains separated by a central valley trough. The mountains originate in France and curve up through Switzerland and into Austria.

Covering more than 60 percent of Switzerland, the Alps are a difficult obstacle to surmount. The range has many high peaks, including the Dufourspitze summit of Monte Rosa (15,203 feet), the Dom (14,913 feet), and the Matterhorn (14,691 feet). All mountains over 6,000 feet in elevation have snow for at least half of the year. In the spring, when the weather turns warm and sunny, some of this snow starts to melt, triggering massive snowslides called avalanches. There are approximately ten thousand avalanches each year in the Alps, with roughly eight thousand of them occurring in February, March, and April. There are also over a thousand glaciers in the Alps, covering approximately 1,000 square miles. One of

The snowy, craggy Matterhorn is one of the highest peaks of the Alps.

these, the Aletsch Glacier, is the largest valley glacier in Europe, measuring nearly 15 miles long and about 85 square miles overall.

With so much snow and ice, the Alps are the hydrographic center of Europe, which means they are the source of many of Europe's waterways. In fact, Europe's two largest rivers, the Rhone and the Rhine, both originate in the Alps. The Rhone cuts across part of southern Switzerland before flowing into France and on to the Mediterranean Sea. The Rhine forms part of the border between Switzerland and its neighbors Austria and Germany before continuing into Germany and on to the North Sea. These and other rivers have cut valleys into the Alps, and today Alpine valleys are prime grazing land for cows. Along with ample water, the richness of the land was part of what attracted many of Switzerland's original settlers.

Another attraction of the Alps is the dry air. Such air is beneficial for people with lung problems, who cannot tolerate damp weather. Consequently, beginning in the nineteenth century, the Swiss built health facilities called sanatoriums in the mountains to accommodate these people. Such facilities continue to attract thousands of sick people to the region, particularly in winter, when other parts of Europe are cold and damp.

Still another attraction to the Alps is its recreational opportunities. Tourists, skiers, and mountain climbers are all drawn to the natural beauty of the Alps and its challenging slopes. To provide people with easier access to the region, the Swiss have built several roads through the Alps—a difficult accomplishment given the often steep terrain and harsh weather. The most heavily traveled of these roads is the Saint Gotthard Pass, the major north-south passage through the mountains. In 1882, the Swiss built a 9.3 mile train tunnel to shelter railway tracks and in 1980 construction began on two 10.5-mile automobile tunnels to protect the road from snow. However, when the pass was first opened in the early thirteenth century, travelers had great difficulty using the route, particularly in winter. Nonetheless, there were no other direct north-south routes at

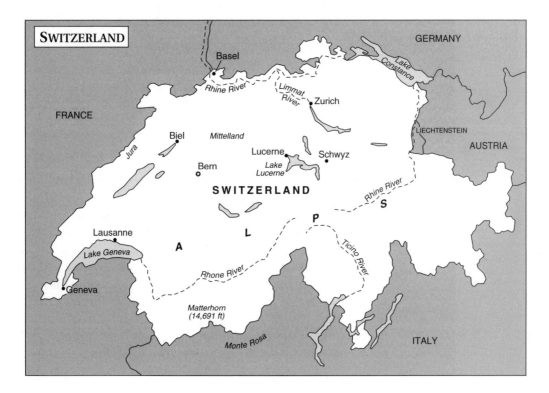

the time. Ancient travelers had to rely on long, narrow, winding passes, most of them cut by rivers, to get over the mountains.

Switzerland has another, less demanding mountain range called the Jura. Cutting across the northwestern edge of Switzerland, it covers approximately 160 miles along the border regions of France and Switzerland but has no peak higher than 5,660 feet. Nonetheless, it still acts as a barrier between groups of people for two main reasons. First, its lower slopes are heavily forested in many places; in fact, the word *jura* means "forest" in ancient Celtic. Second, although the mountains have meadows and plateaus near their crests, they have few rivers, which means that there are no natural passes through the range. Therefore, although the western side of the Jura attracted many early European hunters because of the deer and bears who lived in the forests, few ancient people ventured over the mountains into what is now Switzerland.

THE MITTELLAND

Between the Jura and the Alps lies the Bernese Mittelland, or "Middle Land," a central plateau of rolling hills. Covering approximately 23 percent of Switzerland, it is crisscrossed by

ALTITUDE SICKNESS

Many of Switzerland's mountains are so tall that the human body has difficulty adapting to the lower oxygen levels on their peaks. This can bring on an illness known as acute mountain sickness (AMS), which affects people differently. At its mildest, AMS can cause shortness of breath, coughing, fatigue, muscle weakness, headache, nausea, vomiting, and/or loss of appetite. More serious cases of AMS can involve hypoxia, a condition in which the brain has difficulty functioning and people become confused and disoriented. At its most severe, AMS can cause fluid to develop in the lungs and/or brain. When fluid develops in the lungs, a person can die from drowning; when fluid develops in the brain, the sufferer will hallucinate and fall into a coma before dying. The only cure for AMS is to get down to a lower altitude as quickly as possible. To prevent AMS, one must ascend a mountain gradually, allowing his or her body to adjust to higher and higher levels of altitude. Swiss people are well educated about the causes and symptoms of AMS from a young age.

Lake Geneva marks part of the border between Switzerland and France.

rivers and has over a thousand lakes. At the southwestern and northeastern edges of the Mittelland, respectively, are Lake Constance and Lake Geneva, the two largest lakes in Switzerland. Lake Geneva marks part of the border between Switzerland and France, and Lake Constance encompasses the border separating Switzerland from Austria and Germany. As with Switzerland's mountain ranges, these geographical features attracted settlers but also acted as natural barriers, isolating one group of Swiss people from another.

The Mittelland is a pleasant place to live, but it does have some weather-related challenges. Both Lake Geneva and Lake Constance, for example, often have dense fog during fall and winter. In addition, Lake Geneva frequently experiences a cold northwest wind known as the Bise, which blows across the Mittelland. The counterpart of this wind is the Foehn, or Föhn, a warm southern wind that blows over the Alps and down into its valleys. Both winds are said to make people edgy and restless, although the Foehn is considered the worse of the two.

In the summer, the Mittelland is warm and sunny, with an average temperature of around sixty-five degrees. Because its average altitude is only fifteen hundred feet above sea level, it receives much less snow than the Alps. However, it still gets about forty-five inches of rain each year. Other parts of Switzerland, particularly in Alpine regions, can receive over one hundred inches a year.

Four major European climates collide in Switzerland, making the country's weather unstable. North Atlantic winds from the west bring mild, moist air; Continental winds from the east bring cold, dry air in winter and warm air in summer; Arctic winds from the north bring cold and dry air; and Mediterranean winds from the south bring warm, balmy air. As these winds shift and mix, weather conditions can change dramatically. Warm days can suddenly turn cold, for example, or dry days can turn wet.

Nonetheless, the Mittelland is perfect for growing crops, particularly grain and berries. Although some parts of the Alps are used for agriculture, it is the central plateau that is the farming center of the country. Fertile land and an ample water supply make the farms of the Mittelland extremely valuable today, and they were equally desirable in ancient times. In fact, it was the Mittelland that attracted Switzerland's first settlers.

TRIBAL SETTLERS

The first people to travel into the Mittelland were prehistoric hunters from western Europe following reindeer and bears down from the Jura. Fossils suggest that a few of these people visited the region as early as 350,000 years ago, but large groups of nomadic hunters did not begin to appear until about 30,000 years ago, during a time that archaeologists call the Würm Glacial Period. During this period the land was covered with ice that moved downward from the Alps. This ice would periodically melt in parts of the Mittelland and the Jura, allowing hunters access to these regions.

When the Würm Glacial Period ended, the glaciers melted everywhere but on the high mountains of the Alps. This enabled people to settle permanently in the Mittelland and Alpine valleys, where they formed tribal groups. The first permanent settlements appeared in these regions at least as early as 1500 B.C. Over several hundreds of years, two tribes became more powerful than the rest: the Rhaetians (also called the Rhaeti) and the

Helvetians (or Helvetii). The Rhaetians were part of a broader group of people known as the Etruscans, who originated in northern Italy. The Helvetians were part of a group called the Celts, a warrior people who controlled much of Europe. In Switzerland, the Rhaetians lived on or near several Alpine lakes and controlled a part of the Alps now known as Graubünden; the Helvetians controlled much of the Jura as well as the Mittelland plain between Lakes Constance and Geneva.

Lack of shelter, high altitude, and frigid weather doomed the Roman assault on the Rhaetians in the Great Saint Bernard Pass.

Both groups had to endure assaults from invaders who wanted their land. In 107 B.C., for instance, Romans attacked the Rhaetians after traveling through northern Italy and into the Alps via a route that is today called the Great Saint Bernard Pass. This pass was named after Bernard of Menthon, a monk who provided shelter for travelers along the route in A.D. 1050. The invading Romans, however, had no such shelter. Exposed for days to cold and winds, and unaccustomed to the high altitudes of the Alps, they were so debilitated by their journey that they were unable to conquer Swiss lands.

Tribes coming from what is now Germany had far easier routes into the Mittelland by way of the Jura. Once in central Switzerland, they threatened Helvetian control there. By 58 B.C. the Helvetians had grown so weary of assaults by Germanic tribes that they decided to abandon their lands. After collecting their cattle and belongings, they destroyed their twelve towns and four hundred villages so that the Germanic tribes would not be able to live in them. Then they set out for southern France—a mass of over 368,000 men, women, and children— where they thought they would find ample available land and few people to challenge them.

When they reached the Rhone River, however, they found an encampment of Roman soldiers blocking their way, and a battle broke out. The soldiers were well-trained professional military men who easily forced the Helvetian families to return home. After the conquest, the Roman ruler at the time, Julius Caesar, promised the Helvetians that Rome would protect their lands from Germanic invaders in exchange for making all Helvetian territory part of the Roman Empire. Forty years later, the Rhaetians joined the empire as well, after being defeated in a series of skirmishes with Rome. Nearly all of what is now Switzerland—which the Romans renamed Helvetia—was then under Roman control.

ROMAN INFLUENCES

Switzerland prospered under the Romans for the next two centuries. The Rhaetians and the Helvetians were largely allowed to govern themselves, so they suffered little from Roman rule. Meanwhile, the Roman Empire fortified the region against Germanic invasions by building several military posts and many cities. The most significant of the latter was Aventicum (now the city of Avenches) in western Switzerland, which became the capital of Helvetia. Within the walls of this city— which were four miles in circumference—were many palaces, temples, and arched monuments. The ruins of some of these structures remain today.

Other cities were primarily agricultural. The Romans built fortified farms with irrigation systems, and they brought grapevines from Italy to many of these farms to produce wine. To improve the transport of goods between Italy and Switzerland, they paved mountain passes through the Alps with stones. They also built military fortifications along these roads and posted soldiers to ward off invaders.

In addition to physical improvements, the Romans influenced Swiss culture. One way this influence manifested itself was through language. For example, under Roman rule the Rhaetians began incorporating Latin, the language of Rome, into their own speech, thereby creating the Romance language still used today in parts of Switzerland. Similarly, Rome's name for Switzerland, Helvetia, appears on modern Swiss documents, currency, and stamps. Rome also introduced Christianity to Switzerland. Although the empire itself was opposed to Christianity at that time, one of its military commanders, Mauritius, practiced the religion privately. When he was posted to Switzerland with a legion of defenders, he apparently shared his religion with the people there. Later, however, he was executed for his faith.

GERMANIC INVASIONS

Although Roman occupation brought many new construction projects and ideas to Switzerland, it did not solve the problem of foreign invasions. Beginning in A.D. 259, Germanic tribes launched a series of assaults on Helvetian territory. Their incursions continued for over a hundred years. During this time, Rome faced invasions in other parts of its territory from other tribes. For instance, an eastern tribe called the Huns attacked part of Italy. Forced to defend their empire on many fronts, Roman forces were weakened. By A.D. 400 one Germanic tribe, the Alemanni, succeeded in taking over northern Switzerland after crossing the Rhine River and the Jura.

Violent bullies, the Alemanni killed anyone who would not accept their rule and adopt their language and customs. Villages that resisted Alemanni conquest were destroyed. Meanwhile, another tribe, the Burgundians, took over southwestern Switzerland. The Burgundians were originally from a French-speaking region, and their language is still spoken in the Swiss lands they once occupied. However, little besides their language remains in the region today. Over time, the Burgundians adopted the culture of the Roman Celts who lived in the region they had conquered.

The Alemanni, too, eventually lost control over their lands. In the late fifth and early sixth centuries they were taken over by the Franks, another Germanic tribe. The Alemanni successfully fought off the Franks in the seventh century, but by the eighth century they once again found themselves under Frank rule. At first the Franks divided Switzerland into two kingdoms, Austrasia and Neustria. Then they united their lands under one entity, the Holy Roman Empire, which included much of western Europe. Its emperor, Charlemagne, treated Switzerland as a unified country. For ease of government, however, he portioned it into smaller political regions, first called shires and later cantons; the term *canton* is still used today to refer to one type of Swiss geographical/political unit. Charlemagne allowed the Swiss to manage their own local affairs, and under this system they learned to settle their own disputes.

Holy Roman emperor Charlemagne divided Switzerland into political regions that were later called cantons.

DISPUTES OVER CONTROL

In 814 Charlemagne died and his son, a weak ruler named Ludwig the Pious, barely managed to hold his empire together. When Ludwig died, his three sons fought over control of his lands. Eventually the Holy Roman Empire was divided among them, and Switzerland was divided as well. One son, Ludwig the German, received half of Switzerland; the remainder went to another son, Lothar.

In 1032 the Holy Roman Empire was united again under a strong ruler, Emperor Conrad II, and Switzerland was united again, too. Swiss unity continued throughout the twelfth and thirteenth centuries, but only on the surface. During this time, Swiss nobles from four rival families—the Zahringens, Savoys, Kyburgs, and Habsburgs—plotted independently to take over the land. Each family built fortified cities and castles, choosing geographically strategic positions that helped them expand their domains. At various times, the Zahringen family commanded a substantial area

✚ The Habsburgs

The Habsburg family was one of the most powerful sovereign dynasties in Europe, ruling many European countries from the fifteenth to mid–eighteenth centuries. It first established itself in Switzerland in a castle named Habsburg, or "Hawk's Castle." Within a short time, the family gained strength in Germany and Austria, where many of its members became emperors, grand dukes, dukes, and cardinals. Eventually Habsburgs ruled in Bohemia, Hungary, Bavaria, Poland, parts of Italy, Spain, Brazil, and Mexico. Unlike most other powerful European families, the Habsburgs took over these regions not through warfare but through marriage; Habsburg males typically wooed the daughters of the richest and noblest families. In medieval Austria this practice gave rise to a saying: *Bella gerant alii, tu felix Austria nube*, or Let others wage war: you, fortunate Austria, marry.

between Lakes Constance and Neuchâtel, the Savoys controlled much of western Switzerland, and the Kyburgs controlled much of the northeast.

Meanwhile, the Habsburgs gained dominion over the major east-west trade routes through the Mittelland and access to the Saint Gotthard Pass through the Alps. Their territory also included several important rivers and lakes. With so much power, the Habsburgs gained the favor of the Franks' religious leader, Pope Gregory, who was responsible for choosing the next Holy Roman Emperor. In 1273 Gregory selected the head of the Habsburgs, Rudolf I, for this position.

Swiss Confederacies

As soon as he was crowned emperor, Rudolf started taking land and imposing taxes in order to weaken the Habsburgs' rivals. He also unfairly taxed free peasants, appointing tyrannical bailiffs to collect the money and oversee the laws of the land. By the time Rudolf died in 1291, the peasants were so angry over the bailiffs' cruel treatment that some of them banded together to fight the Habsburgs. The government units established by Charlemagne—the cantons—continued to exist, and they provided rebellious peasants with a way to meet and plan.

The reign of Rudolf I was marred by his efforts to weaken the Habsburgs' rivals.

Three of these cantons—Unterwalden, Schwyz, and Uri, which were known collectively as the Forest Cantons—formed a particularly strong alliance, based in large part on shared concerns related to their lands' geography. The Forest Cantons were adjacent to one another in some wooded Alpine valleys, and together the peasants had to find ways to deal with common problems related to forest management. They had to cooperate to prevent the overcutting of trees and the overgrazing of cattle, for instance, unless they wanted to cause mudslides that would affect their neighbors. Therefore, it was natural for these cantons to feel a strong sense of unity with one another and to feel compelled to join forces against the Habsburgs.

Consequently, on August 1, 1291, the Forest Cantons met near Lake Lucerne to sign a pact against the Habsburgs proclaiming,

> Therefore know all men that the people of the valley of Uri, the democracy of the valley of Schwyz, and the community of the mountaineers of the Lower Valley [Unterwalden], seeing the malice of the age, in order that they may better defend themselves and their own, and better preserve them in proper conditions, have promised in good faith to assist each other with aid, with every counsel and favour, with person and goods, within the valleys and without, with might and main, against one and all, who may inflict upon any one of them any violence, molestation or injury, or may plot any evil against their person or goods. . . . We will accept or receive no judge in the aforesaid valleys, who shall have obtained his office for any price, or for money in any way whatever, or one who shall not be a native or resident with us.[4]

This document marked the foundation of the Swiss Confederation, a group dedicated to protecting its members from tyranny and outsiders and to spreading freedom throughout the land. This confederation eventually became known as the Schweiz, a name derived from the Schwyz canton that participated in the pact; it is from this word that the name *Switzerland* evolved.

Once the confederation was formed, free peasants carrying long pointed sticks called pikes began hiding in the woods to ambush Habsburg knights. Soon larger battles broke out, with soldiers from the two groups engaging in heavily armed conflicts. The Habsburgs responded to this warfare by blockading the peasants' supply routes and by sending additional forces into Switzerland from Habsburg-controlled Austria, but even this was not enough to quell the conflict.

The war between the two groups lasted over 150 years. During this time, more cantons joined the confederation, bringing the total to eight by the end of the fourteenth century. These forces eventually proved too much for the Habsburgs. In 1394 the family signed a five-year peace treaty with the Swiss Confederation, and in 1415 it signed a twenty-year

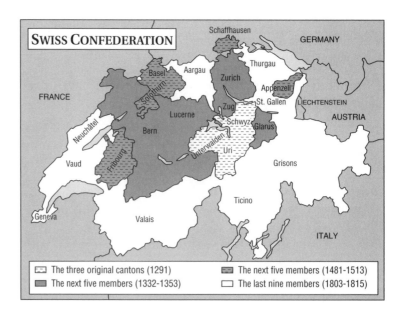

SWISS CONFEDERATION

The three original cantons (1291)
The next five members (1332-1353)
The next five members (1481-1513)
The last nine members (1803-1815)

treaty. At this point, the war officially ended. But with a history of divisiveness and lacking a common enemy to unite its forces, Switzerland's ability to hold itself together was weak. Internal wars soon threatened to divide the country once more.

From a Warring People to a Unified Nation

After signing the 1415 peace treaty with the Habsburgs, the Swiss Confederation looked for other lands to conquer. It had tasted the power and wealth of military conquest, and it wanted more of it. As a result, the confederation not only fought with other countries, but its member cantons fought each other as well. Gradually, as the Swiss became experienced warriors, they eventually learned the destructiveness of war and the benefits of peace. By the twentieth century, this knowledge had affected the way the Swiss managed their military and their government, and changes in these areas brought unity to the Swiss people.

The Burgundian and Swabian Wars

There were several wars on the road to peace and unification, beginning with the conquest of more Habsburg lands between the first and second Habsburg treaties. Once it could no longer usurp Habsburg lands, the Swiss Confederation fought with— and defeated—the duke of Burgundy, Charles the Bold, a powerful opponent. Allied with the Austrians, Charles had been attempting to build an empire from the Mediterranean Sea to the North Sea. Once the Burgundian War was over, the Austrians— part of a group of Habsburgs who had not signed the treaty— attacked Switzerland.

During this conflict, the Austrians allied themselves with the Swabian League, a group of southern German principalities unhappy over Swiss conquests in their territory. The battle consequently became known as the Swabian War. After it ended in 1499, more Swiss cantons decided to join the Swiss Confederation because of its military strength, and by the mid-1500s there were thirteen cantons in all.

Charles the Bold, the duke of Burgundy, was defeated by the Swiss in the Burgundian War.

INTERNAL CONFLICTS

Membership in the Swiss Confederation brought military support, but it was not necessarily a harmonious experience. Internal conflicts often broke out in the group. The first signs of disharmony appeared after the Burgundian War, when some members of the confederation objected to the way that the spoils of war were being divided. Rural villages felt that cities were unfairly getting more spoils than they were. Moreover, cantons that did not belong to the Swiss Confederation but had helped in the war argued that they, too, deserved a share of the spoils. When these cantons petitioned to join the confederation, its existing members could not agree on whether they should be allowed in.

At this point, only the intervention of former Swiss judge Niklaus von Flüe prevented civil war. Von Flüe had retired from public life to live as a holy man in a cave, but he remained a respected figure in Switzerland. Thus, he was asked to mediate in the dispute between rural and city leaders. When negotiations were over, the cantons had agreed to distribute spoils more fairly and decided that any canton willing to end alliances with other groups could join the confederation. Although historians dispute the extent of his influence, von Flüe's work had prevented war, and approximately five centuries later the Catholic Church made him the only Swiss saint.

Although they did not go to war, rural cantons remained unhappy with how wealthy the cities had become. Rural peasants still had to pay taxes to noble landowners, and their farming villages were relatively poor. Chafing under what they considered unfair disadvantages, the rural villages threatened to revolt. However, they found a way to lift themselves out of poverty. During the many battles previously fought by the confederation, Swiss peasants had become skilled soldiers well versed in weaponry. They had also gained a good reputation throughout Europe for their military prowess. Therefore, it was fairly easy for them to find foreign rulers willing to hire them as mercenaries—that is, soldiers who fight strictly for money rather than for a cause.

From the fifteenth to the nineteenth centuries, Swiss mercenaries became a major export for Switzerland, causing problems for the Swiss Confederation. It gave its support to participants in several foreign wars by offering confederation soldiers to help its allies. This meant that in some conflicts there were Swiss soldiers—both hired ones and confederation ones—on both sides, fighting against each other. The confederation addressed this situation by forbidding its citizens from fighting for hire, but many peasants ignored the law having grown too dependent on mercenary money.

RELIGIOUS CONFLICTS

Arguments between rural and city dwellers, poor and rich, were not the only conflicts in Switzerland during this period. There were many religious disagreements not only among the Swiss but also throughout Europe. Much of the conflict stemmed from a protest in Germany by a religious leader named Martin Luther. In 1517 Luther began accusing the Catholic Church of sacrificing Christian principles for money. In particular, he objected to a common practice in the church whereby priests would pardon the sins of people who paid for absolution. Luther proposed a series of church reforms, including the end of paid pardons and a lessening of priests' power over worshipers. When the Catholic Church refused to adopt these changes, Luther's followers started their own religion, which eventually became known as Lutheranism.

As people became exposed to Martin Luther's ideas, they interpreted them in new ways, and soon the religion had inspired several different sects. This was particularly true in Switzerland. In the city of Zurich, for example, a priest named Huldrych Zwingli developed a variation of Lutheranism in which worshipers rather than priests controlled every aspect of the church. In 1523 Zwingli convinced city leaders to abolish all Catholic Church services so that his own religion could flourish. This led to a war between the people of Zurich and those who lived in its surrounding rural areas, where Catholicism

✚ HULDRYCH ZWINGLI

Born in Switzerland in 1484, Huldrych Zwingli studied theology and became a priest in 1506. Shortly thereafter, while working as a chaplain for Swiss mercenaries, he decided to oppose the mercenary system because it pitted one Swiss soldier against another. This brought him both enemies and supporters. Zwingli's views on religion were also controversial. After being appointed priest in Zurich in 1518, he proposed many church reforms, including the removal of religious images from churches and the simplification of religious services. Zwingli also argued that priests should be allowed to marry—which he himself did in 1524. Zwingli promoted his ideas in lectures and writings, thereby inspiring the Swiss Reformation. In 1531, while working as a wartime chaplain, he was killed during a battle near Zurich. Today a stone marks the place where he fell.

*Huldrych Zwingli
proposed many reforms
in the Catholic Church
that helped to inspire
the Swiss Reformation.*

was still the preferred religion. During this war, Zwingli and
many of Zurich's leaders were killed on the battlefield. The vic-
tors cremated Zwingli's body and scattered his ashes as further
punishment, believing that this would keep his soul from find-
ing peace after death.

Another variation on Lutheranism was Calvinism, which developed in the Swiss city of Geneva. Named after its founder, a
German priest named John Calvin, it was a very harsh religion.
Calvin believed that people should behave in very modest
ways, following a strict code of behavior. For instance, he for-
bade his followers to play cards, wear jewelry, dance, or sing
any music other than religious hymns. Girls were not allowed

Highly influential in Geneva, John Calvin developed the strict religion of Calvinism.

to skate, and hairdressers were not allowed to create unusual or showy hairstyles. All worshipers were required to attend church twice on Sunday. In addition, they had to be home by 9:00 P.M. every night. During the day they were required to follow strict dietary rules. For example, people could only eat one meat dish and one vegetable dish per day, and they could never have a pastry.

Calvin wielded great power in Geneva, and to enforce his rules there, he created a church tribunal with twelve civic members who doled out punishments to wrongdoers. Often these punishments were severe. For instance, a Spanish scholar visiting Switzerland was burned to death for publicly criticizing a Calvinist doctrine, and a woman who committed adultery was sewn into a sack and thrown into a river. Within a three-year period, there were fifty-eight executions, seventy-six banishments, and eight to nine thousand prison sentences meted out. There were many lesser punishments as well. For example, a man who called Calvin evil was ordered to carry a torch through city streets clad only in a shirt, stopping in three public squares to tell people that he himself was evil.

THE THIRTY YEARS' WAR

Calvinism and all other religions inspired by Lutheranism are types of Protestantism, a word derived from the fact that Lutheranism began as an act of protest against the Catholic Church. A large number of Swiss people embraced Protestantism because it appealed to their independent natures. However, the spread of Protestantism throughout Europe angered Roman Catholics, and the Holy Roman Empire, which was the seat of Catholicism, took measures to stop it. As a result, a series of religious and political conflicts erupted between the empire and its Protestant towns and principalities. All of these conflicts, from 1618 to 1648, later became known collectively as the Thirty Years' War.

Although Switzerland was loosely under the control of the Habsburg's German Empire, its cantons had the freedom to decide not to take sides in the war, and they stuck to this decision despite severe criticism from countries that wanted their support. As a result, the Thirty Years' War had a major impact on Swiss perceptions of war and the value of unity. Foremost was Switzerland's discovery that remaining neutral had its

✚ JOHN CALVIN

Born in France in 1509, John Calvin studied for the priesthood at the University of Paris before switching to law school. While a law student, he became involved in a movement dedicated to church reform. When the French government tried to suppress the reformists, Calvin moved to Switzerland. In the city of Basel, he studied theology and wrote the *Institutes*, which outlined his religious beliefs. Published in several versions—the last of which appeared in 1560—it is one of the major works of Protestantism. *Institutes* also attracted the attention of a preacher in Geneva, who invited Calvin to visit him in 1536. By 1541 Calvin had settled in Geneva permanently, transforming it into a town guided by his beliefs. He established an academy there to train ministers, worked as a minister himself, and wrote extensively, but all of his activities led to poor health, and he died in 1564 at age fifty-five.

economic benefits. With other countries too embroiled in battles to tend their farms, Switzerland made a substantial profit as the primary food supplier in the region. Its mercenaries were also in demand, and this too brought money into Swiss coffers. Had Switzerland officially supported the war, it would have had to provide soldiers to its allies for free. Instead, however, a country that needed Swiss soldiers had to pay for them. Switzerland profited as well by accepting refugees from France, who brought with them money and skills. The refugees were especially good at making watches and jewelry and were expert traders and bankers—all talents that are still associated with the Swiss today.

Switzerland benefited even more when the Thirty Years' War ended in 1648. As part of the treaty that resolved the conflicts, the Habsburgs agreed to relinquish all claims to Switzerland and make it a free land. Ironically, with this freedom came dissent. As in the past, without a common enemy, the Swiss could not remain unified. Individual cities looked out only for themselves; likewise, groups of peasants took up arms against the nobles who controlled their land.

In many places, the peasants' complaints of unfair treatment were justified. In the city of Bern, for example, peasants were not allowed to do their shopping in the marketplace until upper- and middle-class people and their servants were finished. Peasants were also not allowed to own houses, even if they had the money to buy them. Because of such mistreatment, peasant revolts became common in Switzerland.

New religious wars broke out in the country as well. Some of their causes seemed trivial. For instance, one war started because people disagreed on whether Catholics or Protestants should be given the task of building a new road. Another war was threatened because someone wanted to carry a Catholic cross in a street parade and Protestants objected.

With Switzerland once again in such internal disarray, foreigners realized that the country was ripe for invasion. The first to act was Napoléon Bonaparte, who led the armies of France. He marched into Bern on March 5, 1798, looted the city's treasures, and established a stronghold there. Within days, ten Swiss cantons had surrendered to France. The three Forest Cantons, however, remained steadfast. They fought a fierce battle against the French but were eventually defeated in September 1798.

Taking advantage of religious strife, Napoléon's army attacked and defeated Switzerland in 1798.

NAPOLÉON'S INFLUENCE

Switzerland now belonged to the French. Renamed the Helvetic Republic, it was not left whole. A few southern pieces of it were given to Italy, also controlled by France, and some of the southwest was made part of France. The rest of Switzerland was divided into twenty-three cantons.

Napoléon then set up a centralized government to take charge of them all. His idea was that the Swiss people would be responsible for their own affairs, with all cantons working together. But Napoléon was obviously unfamiliar with Swiss divisiveness. As in the past, the cantons proved unable to cooperate with one another. They quarreled constantly, and Napoléon eventually became disgusted with them. In 1803 he returned Switzerland to its original form of government, reestablishing the Swiss Confederation so that the cantons functioned separately again. However, he retained jurisdiction over the land until he was forced to abdicate his throne in 1814.

In September of that year, the four countries primarily responsible for the overthrow of Napoléon—Austria, Prussia, Russia, and Great Britain—as well as Sweden, Portugal, and Spain, sent representatives to Vienna, Austria, to determine how Napoléon's lands would be reorganized. Called the Congress of Vienna, this assembly decided that Switzerland should be an independent country. Its twenty-three cantons would be allowed to function separately, providing they maintained a loose form of federal government. The congress also reestablished Switzerland's borders, giving it back some of the territories lost during Napoléon's reign but also taking away others, so that, in the end, Switzerland's borders appeared just as they do today. In addition, because it was in a strategic military location the congress decreed that Switzerland should be neutral in all future foreign wars.

CIVIL WAR

As with Switzerland's own decision to remain neutral during the Thirty Years' War, this decree led to peace and prosperity. A period of economic growth began, and along with it came the modernization of farms and factories. In particular, the Swiss adopted mechanized spinning machines used elsewhere in Europe to help the cotton industry, and eventually they decided to start making these machines themselves. By 1832 Switzerland was a major supplier of spinning machines throughout Europe.

Soon, however, Switzerland's economic growth was threatened by the cantons' continuing inability to work together. Each canton created its own laws and currency, and disagreements among cantons were common. In addition, new fights broke out between peasants and nobles, rural villagers and city dwellers, Catholics and Protestants. The federal government did nothing to quell local disturbances. In fact, rancor among federal leaders only fueled regional disputes.

By 1847 discord in the country had grown so severe that civil war broke out. The trigger was a religious dispute, but many other disagreements were brought into play as cantons formed into two conflicting groups, one Roman Catholic and the other Protestant. Though the war lasted only twenty-five days and resulted in just seventy-eight casualties, it had a lasting effect on the country. Afterward, the Swiss people realized that they had to find a way to unite despite their differences. In 1848 they created a new constitution, modeled after the one in the United States.

SWISS GOVERNMENT

This constitution—with a few minor changes—is still in effect today and continues to unite the country. The document established a Federal Assembly consisting of two legislative bodies, similar to the U.S. House of Representatives and the U.S. Senate. They are called the National Council and the Council of States. The National Council has two hundred elected members, each of whom serves a four-year term, and the Council of States has forty-six members, selected by the local governments of the cantons. There is also an executive body called the Federal Council or the Cabinet, whose seven elected representatives serve four-year terms. Each of these representatives is responsible for a different government department: defense, transportation, energy, justice, the economy, finance, foreign affairs, and interior affairs. Each year one member of this group is elected by the others to be president of the Federal Council and preside over their meetings.

Meanwhile, the cantons are in charge of education, public health, law enforcement, and taxes on a level similar to U.S. states. The 1848 constitution established twenty-five cantons — today there are twenty-six—each functioning independently but overseen by the federal government. Three of these cantons are

Each canton in Switzerland has its own parliament. The parliament building in Bern is shown here.

so small that they are considered half-cantons, with only half the voting power as the rest. Regardless of size, each canton has its own parliament, with a varying number of representatives depending on population. The terms of service for these representatives also vary according to each canton. Within each canton are smaller political units called communes, or *Gemeinde*, which function on a level similar to U.S. city governments. Communes range in size from 109 square miles (such as the Bagnes commune in the canton of Valais) to just 0.1 square mile (the Ponte Teresa commune in the canton of Ticino). Each commune has its own assembly to deal with local concerns, including forest management, road repair, and fire services.

Whereas in the United States there are two large political parties and only a few minor ones, in Switzerland there are about a dozen parties of equal size. These include the Radical Democratic Party, the Social Democratic Party, the Christian Democratic People's Party, and the Swiss People's Party. Each party espouses a slightly different set of beliefs, but people who belong to a party are encouraged to remain independently minded. This philosophy has helped strengthen the country's sense of unity because membership in a political party is not seen as a way to band together against others but as a way to participate in the political process and express varying viewpoints. From the outset, the Swiss constitution recognized that the only way to get Switzerland's people to work together was to give them a great deal of freedom within a loosely structured government. Every aspect of Swiss political life retains this element.

The constitution also recognized that Switzerland had the best chance of remaining unified if it was not torn apart by involvement in foreign wars. By the time the constitution was crafted, Switzerland was made up of people whose ancestors came from France, Germany, Austria, Italy, and many other parts of Europe. Therefore, the loyalties of the country would naturally be divided in any European conflict. Consequently, the constitution decreed that Switzerland would remain neutral in all foreign wars. It also permanently banned the exportation of mercenaries.

A STRONG MILITARY

Many historians have called the establishment of the 1848 Swiss constitution the turning point in Switzerland's history.

Although a few minor disagreements occurred after this time, the country never again experienced the internal conflicts that had for so long been an integral part of Swiss life. Even in the twentieth century, when other European countries fought in World Wars I and II, Switzerland remained at peace internally. It also remained neutral despite being surrounded by combatants, gaining a reputation as a safe haven for foreigners escaping the battlefield.

During World War II, the Swiss fortified their borders to prevent wartime invasions of their neutral country.

This does not mean, however, that Switzerland was without a strong military during the World Wars. In fact, the country so feared wartime invasions that it worked diligently during these periods to fortify its borders and establish a trained army. Bridges, tunnels, and roads into Switzerland were rigged to explode should an enemy try to cross them, and all able-bodied adult males in Switzerland were ready to fight at a moment's notice if necessary. During one particularly perilous time during World War II, the country was able to mobilize 850,000 men to patrol its borders.

Working together to form a strong, defensive military further increased Switzerland's sense of unity. Protecting their land from the threat of invasion gave the Swiss people a common cause. Even today, Switzerland still maintains fortified borders and a strong army. Bridges, tunnels, and roads are equipped with devices that will enable them to be blown up if the need arises, and some form of military service is mandatory among Swiss males.

At the age of twenty, each man must report to a military facility unless he has a physical disability. There, he undergoes fifteen weeks of military training before being sent home with some weaponry and military supplies, including a gas mask. From this point on, he must be prepared to report to active military duty within forty-eight hours of being called. To keep his military skills fresh in the meantime, he must regularly practice target shooting with a rifle he maintains himself. He must also attend a three-week military training course once every two years. These requirements continue even after a man is transferred into the military reserve at age thirty-two. Men in the reserve can still be called for active duty, but only after every eligible male younger than age thirty-two has already been called.

In Switzerland enough bomb shelter space exists to accommodate every Swiss citizen.

When a man who is a regular soldier reaches age forty-two or an officer reaches fifty-two, he is transferred from the military reserve into the civil service. This requires him to undergo

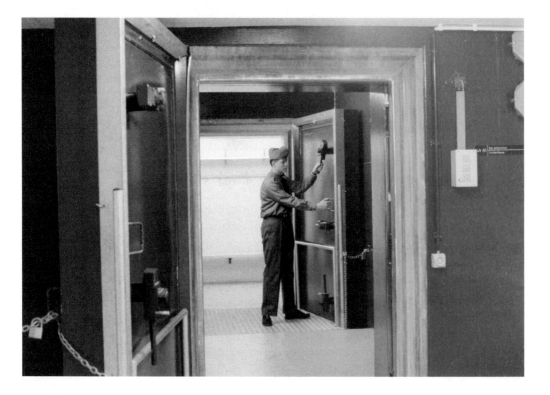

more training because the civil service comprises individuals skilled in specific jobs that support the military in times of war. As of 1991, younger men have had the right to choose civil service as an alternative to military service, but only if they exhibit strong moral objections to war. Both kinds of service do not end until a man reaches the age of sixty. After that, a man cannot be called to active duty, but he is still expected to keep his rifle in good repair and be ready to defend his home.

There are also approximately thirty-five hundred full-time professional Swiss soldiers. Again, they are all male. Women who want to serve in the military can volunteer, but they are kept separate from male military units and would not be allowed to fight on the front lines in times of war. They can, however, assist in getting people to bomb shelters should a state of emergency be called. Enough bomb shelter space currently exists in Switzerland to house every citizen. Most are located beneath commercial buildings because, for the past several years, all new construction has had to include a subterranean bomb shelter.

There are also many underground emergency hospitals and storage rooms filled with nonperishable food and other supplies. The entrances to these facilities are well disguised. For example, one mountainside facility is camouflaged with fake tree stumps. As travel writer Mark Honan says,

> It's a sobering thought, as you explore the [Swiss] countryside, to realise that those apparently undisturbed mountains and lakes hide a network of military installations and storage depots. The message that comes across today is the same as that dealt out by the country's fearless mercenaries of centuries ago: don't mess with the Swiss.[5]

As Honan suggests, Switzerland's history of conflict has well prepared the nation for any act of aggression. Even when the world is not at war, the Swiss are ready to protect themselves from invasion. Their history has taught them to distrust any period of calm and to be ever watchful of their neighbors. At the same time, they have learned the benefits of peace and are therefore willing to hold their combative natures in check. Whereas the Swiss were once among the most warring people in Europe, today they believe that no conflict is worth destroying the unity they worked so hard to build.

3

LAND OF PEACE AND PROSPERITY

The Swiss have prospered financially from their position of neutrality. Once they adopted this position, they no longer had to spend money on foreign wars. Moreover, Switzerland became a safe haven for war refugees from other countries, many of whom came with wealth and valuable skills. As a result, modern Switzerland has a strong economy and productive citizens. These two characteristics have enabled the country not only to improve itself but to provide aid to other countries as well.

PEACE ORGANIZATIONS

In fact, Switzerland is the birthplace of one of the largest aid organizations in the world: the International Red Cross. This humanitarian agency has representatives in almost every country, and in times of war it provides aid to the injured, checks on the condition of prisoners of war, and provides soldiers with relief supplies and mail from home. In times of peace the organization helps victims of natural disasters, provides first-aid training, runs blood-donation drives, and generally works to prevent and relieve human suffering. Its international operations are overseen by a committee of twenty-five Swiss citizens.

The founder of the Red Cross, grain merchant Jean-Henri Dunant, traveled to an Italian battlefield in 1859 to discuss business with French emperor Napoléon III. While there, he witnessed the horrors of war firsthand. Travel writer Erika Schumacher offers a glimpse of Dunant's experience:

> He found himself in the middle of one of the bloodiest battles in history [the Battle of Solferino]—33,000 casualties on the first day alone. Dunant was wearing a white suit appropriate to an imperial audience [i.e., a meeting with Napoléon] when he threw himself into washing wounds and generally helping as casualties poured in at the rate of 55 per minute. After two days and nights with-

out sleep, the man in the now thoroughly bloodied white suite was a legend.[6]

When he returned to Switzerland, Dunant published an account of what he had witnessed, entitled *A Souvenir of Solferino*. This work argued for the creation of an organization that would help all wounded soldiers regardless of their political affiliation. To gain support for such an organization, Dunant toured Europe lecturing on the horrors of war. Eventually he persuaded representatives from several European countries to meet in Geneva, Switzerland, to discuss his proposals. This resulted in the signing of the first Geneva Convention, an international treaty, in 1864.

Then called the Convention for the Amelioration of the Wounded in Time of War, the Geneva Convention has been amended several times since 1864; for instance, in 1929 provisions were added to protect prisoners of war from harm. Today over 150 countries, including the United States, have agreed to abide by the conditions of the Geneva Convention. The treaty establishes specific wartime rules. First, no medical facility should be destroyed or captured. Second, no civilian giving aid to the wounded should be harmed. Third, all injured people should be treated with equal care and concern, regardless of their political alliance. Fourth, the symbol of the Red Cross—a red "plus sign" against a background of white—should be used to designate personnel, supplies, vehicles, and buildings deserving of protection. Countries who

JEAN-HENRI DUNANT

Born in Geneva in 1828, Jean-Henri Dunant not only founded the Red Cross but also the World's Young Men's Christian Association (YMCA). However, all of his activities to promote peace and fellowship—which included the promotion of the first Geneva Convention—caused him to neglect his business affairs. By 1867 Dunant was bankrupt and consequently left Geneva. He lived much of his remaining life in poverty and obscurity, although he did continue to donate time to various political and social causes. In 1895, a journalist tracked him down in Heiden, Switzerland, and again brought him to the attention of the world. People responded by showering Dunant with cash prizes and awards. In 1901 he became the co-winner of the first Nobel Peace Prize ever awarded. He died nine years later.

have signed the Geneva Convention have agreed to abide by these rules.

Geneva has been the site of other peace meetings as well. After World War I, for example, an organization called the League of Nations established its headquarters in Geneva, where it worked to resolve disputes between countries as a way to prevent future wars. It dissolved, however, during the 1930s, largely because it lacked the support of the United States and had no power to enforce its laws. After World War II, a similar organization was formed with the full support of the United States and 50 other countries, including China, Russia, and Great Britain. Called the United Nations, it held its first meeting in 1945 and remains a strong organization today, with 185 member countries. Representatives from each country work together to prevent wars from starting or stop wars already in progress.

The European headquarters for the United Nations is located in Geneva.

Because Switzerland is a neutral country, it is not a member of the United Nations, which sometimes takes sides in disputes. However, the Swiss support the organization by providing it with its European headquarters in Geneva.

BANKING

Switzerland has the economic resources to supply such facilities largely because of its banking industry. The country attracts investors from all over the world. There are two main reasons for this attraction. First, because Switzerland refuses to become involved in wars, investors see it as a safe place to invest their money. Second, the Swiss allow people to bank in complete anonymity, without asking questions about the source of investors' money.

Crédit Suisse, one of many Swiss banks, attracts investors from all over the world.

Ever since World War II, Swiss bank accounts have been identified by numbers rather than by names. This practice began so that Germans could hide money from the Nazis who took over their country and seized its assets, but it also made it possible for Nazis to hide the money they stole. Much of this money remains in Switzerland. In fact, in 1997 an incident called the Nazi Gold Scandal occurred when it was discovered that the Swiss banking industry had roughly $57 million in inactive accounts and had failed to track down the owners; most of these accounts are believed to have been opened by German Jews prior to World War II.

Swiss banks also contain the funds of modern dictators and criminals. For instance, the deposed dictator of Mali, Moussa Traore, deposited at least $1 billion in Switzerland, even though his country is one of the poorest in the world. The source of this money is unclear. In recent years, Switzerland has passed new laws that require bankers to cooperate with police investigating the illegal activities. However, as Mark Honan points out, it is still relatively easy for criminals to hide money in Swiss banks:

In practice, anybody can still open a Swiss bank account, numbered or otherwise. All you have to do is sign a form declaring that the money is rightfully yours. Responding to such a question with an untruth would hardly cause great pangs of conscience in the average underworld boss.[7]

Swiss banks continue to bring in money from a variety of sources, which they then loan for a fee or invest to increase their holdings. Through such means, Swiss bankers have made their country one of the richest in Europe and have provided the wherewithal for many of Switzerland's humanitarian efforts as well as for everyday needs such as road construction, building improvements, and educational programs. Over eleven hundred banks are headquartered in Switzerland, with approximately four thousand branches throughout the country and additional branches throughout the world. The five biggest Swiss banks are the Union Bank of Switzerland, the Swiss Bank Corporation, Crédit Suisse, Swiss Volksbank, and Bank Leu. Although Geneva is the center of the banking industry, all cantons have a large number of banks—so many, in fact, that, according to Honan, "In most cantons there are more banks than dentists."[8]

TOURISM

Over 60 percent of all Swiss workers are employed in banking and financial services or in other service industries. One of the largest of these service industries is tourism, which has been a major asset to the Swiss economy since the Middle Ages. At that time, Europeans began to believe that soaking in natural mineral springs in certain places, like the town of Baden, would cure them of various ills. Health spas were built in such locations to bring in tourist money. This was also the case with sanatoriums in the Swiss Alps, where the air is said to cure respiratory ailments.

In the nineteenth century, additional tourist dollars started coming into Switzerland from British sightseers. They were first attracted to the region via the efforts of Albert Smith, who put on a show about mountaineering at the Egyptian Hall in Piccadilly, London. Smith's show featured information about France's Mont Blanc along with imported, fully costumed Swiss mountaineers and Saint Bernard dogs, famed for guiding lost Alpine travelers to shelters. After England's queen Victoria

visited Smith's show twice, it became the rage in London, and
many people decided it would be fashionable to travel to
Switzerland to see its mountains.

The first British sightseers went to the Swiss Alps only in the
summer, often as part of organized tours, because they falsely
believed that the mountains would be too harsh in winter. After 1864, however, they changed their opinion. According to
some stories, this change occurred after a hotel owner in Saint
Moritz, a mountain town in eastern Switzerland, offered free
lodgings to any Englishman willing to give Alpine winters a try.
Those who accepted his offer found that the weather was quite
pleasant on the lower mountain slopes and in the Alpine valleys. However, Swiss hotel owners feared their reputation as a
good tourist destination would be ruined when some of the visitors complained about Swiss food. One of these visitors wrote,

*In the nineteenth
century, the Swiss Alps
attracted many British
sightseers, including
this group of hikers.*

The great drawback [in the Swiss Alps] is the want of good food. The milk and the bread and the butter are good, but the meat is bad. . . . For three months the only vegetables that we had were potatoes. In fact a person coming here for health gains greatly as regards climate but loses greatly for want of good food and ordinary home comforts.[9]

Fortunately for Switzerland's economy, most sightseers ignored such criticisms, and today the country's hotels and restaurants are typically praised by tourists. In fact, as a travel destination, the country is one of the most popular in the world. About 80 percent of all tourists who visit Switzerland each year are European, and nearly 65 percent of these people

THE CHOCOLATE INDUSTRY

Although chocolate originated in Central America in ancient times and was not transported to Europe until 1528, it was the Swiss who first popularized the chocolate bar. Prior to their involvement with the confection, chocolate was enjoyed only as a hot beverage. The first person to add milk to chocolate, thereby creating what is today known as milk chocolate, was Daniel Peter of Switzerland (1836–1919). Rodolphe Lindt of Switzerland (1855–1909) was the first person to use a process called conching to aerate the chocolate as

it was mixed, a technique which greatly enhanced the texture of chocolate bars. In 1819 François-Louis Cailler (1796–1852) became the first person in Switzerland to build a factory dedicated to the production of chocolate bars. Other notable Swiss chocolate manufacturers include Philippe Suchard (1797–1884), Henri Nestlé (1814–1890), and Jean Tobler (1830–1905). Today the United States rather than Switzerland produces the most chocolate bars per year; Switzerland is tenth. However, the Swiss consume more chocolate per year than any other people—roughly 11.3 kilograms per person.

Each Swiss person consumes about 11.3 kilograms of chocolate per year.

spend at least one night in the Alps. By some estimates, the Alps receive 120 million visitors a year.

AGRICULTURE

Another source of revenue for Switzerland is agriculture. Prior to World War II, over 60 percent of the Swiss made their living from agriculture. Today, however, only about 6 percent are agricultural workers because most farms are large and mechanized. Many farms produce wines, grains, grasses, and berry products, but the primary agricultural exports of Switzerland are dairy products, including cheese and milk chocolates. The country sells over $16 million worth of chocolate abroad each year via companies like Tobler, Lindt, and Nestlé Foods. The Swiss also sell several types of cheese, including Emmentaler and Gruyère. These two cheeses are nearly identical, with large holes created by bubbles that occur during the milk fermentation process. However, it is Emmentaler that most people call "Swiss cheese."

Swiss cattle are known for their superior milk.

Because Switzerland sells so much cheese and chocolate, the country's dairy industry is vitally important. As one seventeenth-century resident of the city of Lucerne wrote, "The products that can be obtained from milk and from cattle are the precious and divine materials of our mountains and bring gold, silver, and much wealth into our country."[10] Hundreds of dairies are located throughout Switzerland; in fact, almost every rural village has at least one dairy, supplied with milk not only by its own cows but by the cows of farmers throughout the area. This milk is so superior that people in other countries have not been able to duplicate it. According to Erika Shumacher, "Even identical processing cannot achieve the flavour imparted by the Alpine herbs which the cows eat on the high pastures during the summer months."[11] Therefore, although Germany,

France, Austria, Finland, Argentina, Australia, and the United States make "Swiss" cheese, many gourmets consider these cheeses inferior to genuine Swiss cheese.

INDUSTRY

Dairying and cattle raising account for over 70 percent of all Swiss agricultural income, but the amount of money earned through agriculture of any kind is far less in comparison to that made by the industrial sector. Over the years, industrial jobs have gradually replaced agricultural ones, even in rural areas. By the end of the nineteenth century over 90 percent of Switzerland's population was rural, but the majority of these people worked in textile or chemical factories.

Today over 34 percent of the Swiss are involved in the manufacture and/or export of industrial goods, which include machinery and equipment, textiles and apparel, chemicals and drugs, and watches. Of these, the Swiss watch and clock manufacturing industry is most famous throughout the world. The Swiss have been considered expert watchmakers since the sixteenth century, when French refugees skilled in the craft settled in and around Geneva. From there, the industry spread into the Jura mountains, where it became an integral part of the social structure of the region. In 1871 a Russian prince named Peter Kropotkin wrote about this watchmaking society, saying,

> In a little valley in the Jura hills, there is a succession of small towns and villages of which the French-speaking population was at that time entirely employed in the various branches of watchmaking: whole families used to work in small workshops. In one of them I found . . . [a man who] sat among a dozen young men who were engraving lids of gold and silver watches. I was asked to take a seat on a bench, or a table, and soon we were all engaged in a lively conversation upon socialism, government or no government, and the coming [political] congresses.[12]

Today's Swiss watchmakers typically employ factory methods to produce goods on a much larger scale than in the past. Over 70 million watches and watch parts are manufactured in Switzerland each year. Most of these watches are expensive. Swiss watches account for about 90 percent of the highest priced watches sold each year throughout the world.

Switzerland also brings in revenue through the pharmaceutical industry. Several of the world's biggest pharmaceutical companies are headquartered in Switzerland, including Hoffman La Roche, and they have developed many new vitamin products and medicines that are in demand throughout the world. Other major Swiss companies manufacture electronics and machinery, particularly large, heavy equipment. Over 45 percent of all Swiss exports fall into these categories. The Swiss are particularly known for their train technology, having built the first electric-track railway as well as advanced power-station equipment and hydroelectric power plants.

Swiss watchmakers produce 90 percent of the highest priced watches sold throughout the world.

TRANSPORTATION

Switzerland's advances in train technology came as a result of its attempts to solve transportation problems in its own country. Switzerland must devote a lot of its financial resources to maintaining its roads because it has more automobiles per resident than most other European countries. This situation has led to heavy traffic congestion, particularly in mountain tourist areas in the summer, and the Swiss designed an extensive railway system to help alleviate this problem. Over 99 percent of railway tracks are electrified. Some trains are equipped to carry heavy trucks, but others are passenger trains on underground railways. More than half of all trains are operated by the federal government; the remainder are run by one of seventy-five private railroads, many co-owned by cantons. Trains link major cities together, and most major airports are linked to rail lines as well.

The Swiss are now considered experts in the field of transportation and are in demand internationally. In her guidebook *Culture Shock! Switzerland*, Shirley Eu-Wong reports that the expertise of Swiss engineers is due both to the geographical challenges in Switzerland and to experience:

The Swiss built an extensive electric railway system to help reduce traffic.

Air pollution, caused primarily by the abundance of cars, has damaged approximately 35 percent of Swiss forests.

One of the prime reasons Switzerland excels in this field is because the Swiss have had many years of experience. The country's difficult topography demands ingenious planning and construction for roads and railways, with a view to preserving the panoramic beauty of its landscape. Many contractors can lay an asphalt road across a desert plain, but as soon as it starts to get hilly, it pays to call in a Swiss firm. . . . From the gigantic dam at Itaipu on the Amazon [River] in South America to the flyover bridges in Alexandria in Egypt, Swiss builders are relentlessly contributing their share in enlivening the national economy.[14]

ENVIRONMENTALISM

The many roads and cars in Switzerland have led to serious environmental problems. Approximately 35 percent of Swiss forests have been seriously damaged by air pollution, primarily from automobiles. Of these damaged forests, 42 percent are in tourist areas and therefore threaten tourism revenue. For the sake of its economy and environmental well-being, Switzerland has begun to pass laws governing the maintenance and manufacture of cars to reduce their polluting emissions.

In the year 2000, cities also began to promote the practice of car-sharing as a way to protect the environment. At train stations and other key locations along mass transit routes, cars are available for short-term rent, making it possible for a person to use a car for only a few minutes or a few hours. The car need not be left at the same place it was picked up; drop-off points are available throughout the city. Moreover, no attendants are necessary to handle the transaction. Participants in the car-sharing program have an electronic credit card that they use to open the car's door and start the engine, and this card keeps track of their driving time.

Because of the ease of this system, many urban workers use car-sharing to get them from the train station to their office. According to Swiss studies, the creation of this system immediately increased the use of public transportation among users from 20 percent of the time to 90 percent of the time. Consequently, other countries have decided to use Switzerland as a model for developing their own car-sharing programs in order to reduce air pollution.

The Swiss have also taken steps to reduce pollution caused by waste disposal. Paper, aluminum, and plastic recycling is practiced widely throughout the country, and 60 percent of all glass bottles are recycled. To encourage recycling, most cantons charge a substantial fee for collecting nonrecyclable waste. The country has also banned the use of several environmentally harmful materials, including detergents that contain phosphates. When phosphates build up in lakes and rivers, they can throw the ecosystem of these environments out of balance, causing some plants to thrive at the expense of others. At very high levels, phosphates can be toxic to animals and people.

Another common environmental problem in Switzerland is the destruction of wilderness areas in order to increase tourist revenue. For example, owners of mountain resorts sometimes destroy forests while expanding their facilities. Recently a group of Swiss resort owners voluntarily agreed to make improvements on their existing facilities rather than demolish them to build newer, larger resorts, specifically so they would limit their impact on the surrounding environment. Meanwhile, the Swiss

WILDLIFE EXTINCTION

Prior to the seventeenth century, the woods in the Graubünden region of Switzerland had numerous brown bears, deer and stags, and ibex (a species of wild mountain goat). In the seventeenth century, however, hunters killed the last of the ibex there—not for food but for potions and spells—because the Swiss believed that ibex meat possessed magical powers. In the nineteenth century, the brown bear population was extensively overhunted for both its fur and its meat, and in 1904 the last brown bear in all of Switzerland

was killed in Graubünden. By 1914, when the Swiss National Park was established in the region, all of the stags in the area had also been killed. Stags have moved into the area in recent years, but bears remain absent, and the few ibex placed there by conservationists have left for other regions.

Attempts by conservationists to revitalize the ibex population have failed.

government has passed several forestation laws to prevent the destruction of healthy woodlands by limiting how many trees can be cut in certain areas.

The Swiss people's ability to unite in coming up with feasible solutions to environmental problems is a measure of how far they have come in modern times. Although there are still disagreements over difficult issues, as a whole the Swiss understand that too much strife would threaten the peace and prosperity they have worked so hard to build.

4

Modern Swiss People

Although its early history of divisiveness eventually led to unity, Switzerland still has scars from the experience. Its people speak several different languages, and different parts of the country have different priorities and lifestyles. Amidst such diversity, it has been a challenge for the Swiss to maintain their sense of unity. At the same time, experience with diversity has given the Swiss a keen awareness of multicultural issues, an asset in working with other countries in humanitarian and peacekeeping efforts.

Linguistic Diversity

The most obvious holdover from Switzerland's past conflicts is the many languages spoken in the country. Invaders and refugees from Germany, Austria, Italy, and France all retained their own languages even after they became Swiss, and they continue to speak these languages today. As a result, there are four national languages in Switzerland.

The most common is German. It is spoken in 74 percent of the country, primarily in the northeast and central regions. There are actually two types of German used. One is High German, the standard written and spoken German taught throughout Europe and the United States. The second is Swiss German, also called Schwyzerdütsch or Schwyzertütsch. This is an oral language, and as such, it is rarely written down. More akin to Dutch than German, it is used primarily in private conversations among friends and at home. The language varies slightly from region to region because it has no written standard.

French is the next most common language in Switzerland. It is spoken in 20 percent of the country, primarily in the west. Italian is third, spoken in 4 percent of the country and heard mostly in the south. The fourth language is a peasant dialect called Rhaeto-Romance, which developed after the first Roman invasion of Swiss lands in about 107 B.C. This dialect is spoken in 1

percent of the country, and only in the southeast. It is particularly popular in the canton of Graubünden, where about a third
of the population speaks Romance. The remainder of the people in this canton—which is the largest in the country geographically, occupying about one-sixth of Switzerland and
including about twenty-eight hundred square miles—speak
Italian and/or Swiss German.

Most Swiss speak at least one of the national languages,
and usually three. A majority also know some English. As
Shirley Eu-Wong reports, "Through the years, the Swiss have
realised that the vast majority of the world speaks (or at least
understands) English. It is therefore quite common to find
Swiss university students trilingual and very glib in English."[15]

Eu-Wong also reports that people's language skills depend
not only on which region of the country they inhabit but also
on whether they live in an urban or rural setting. City dwellers
are more likely to grow up speaking several languages or, as
adults, to typically pay to attend one of Switzerland's many language schools. She says, "Where you live will greatly determine
which language you speak. In larger or simply more touristy
cities, you will find English spoken at its best. In smaller towns
or villages, it is natural that the local language is the only means
of communicating."[16]

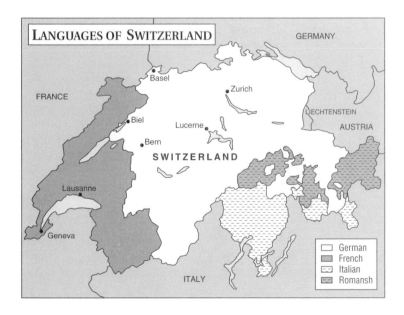

Because of the country's language diversity, the Swiss government prints all of its documents in High German, French, and Italian. These three languages also appear on all bank notes. German is the preferred language for people in business and the civil service, and it is used for most newspapers and magazines as well. English-language newspapers, magazines, and television programs are also widely available. Of the more than a dozen television channels in Switzerland, some are devoted to broadcasting in French, others in Italian, and still others in Romance. However, most use either High German or Swiss German. Interestingly, the latter is primarily used for sports broadcasts, the former for serious news broadcasts.

SWISS EMIGRANTS

Over the years, several Swiss groups have left their country to settle in America. These include the Mennonites, a religious group from Zurich. Named after their leader, Menno Simmons, they eventually split into several sects, including the Amish. Today both the Mennonites and the Amish continue to live in Pennsylvania, where they first settled.

Another Swiss group to come to America founded the city of New Glarus, Wisconsin. After a long journey by land and sea, over one hundred Swiss people from the canton of Glarus established the Wisconsin colony, where many of them became cheesemakers. Today the state continues to be known for its cheese.

Individual emigrants from Switzerland also made their mark in America. Of these, perhaps the most famous is Louis Chevrolet. Louis Chevrolet (1879–1941) was a Swiss race-car driver who immigrated to the United States in 1900. At first he competed in races as the representative of a car manufacturer, but later he designed his own cars. He built the first Chevrolet car in 1911 with William Durant,

to whom he sold all rights to his product in 1915. Nonetheless, a division of General Motors, which worked with Durant to produce a line of Chevrolet cars, continues to bear Louis Chevrolet's name.

Swiss emigrant Louis Chevrolet built the first Chevrolet car with William Durant in 1911.

RELIGIOUS DIVERSITY

As with language, a person's religion is also influenced by location. About 46 percent of the country is Roman Catholic, 40 percent is Protestant, and the remainder is either nondenominational or some other religion, such as Buddhism. About three-tenths of a percent of the country practices Judaism; only twenty towns in Switzerland have thriving Jewish communities.

Italian-speaking regions in southern Switzerland are Catholic strongholds while French-speaking regions are primarily Protestant. Within the Protestant religion, different sections of the country adhere to different sects. In German-speaking regions, for instance, most Protestants belong to the Reformed Church or Evangelical-Reformed Church, whose tenets are based on the teachings of the sixteenth-century religious leader Huldrych Zwingli. In French-speaking regions, most Protestants adhere to a form of the religion established by John Calvin, another sixteenth-century religious leader. Once called Calvinism, today it is typically referred to as Scottish Presbyterianism.

Switzerland has also had many problems with religious cults in modern times. Because of its reputation as a safe haven, the country attracts foreigners who fear religious persecution. Nonetheless, the Swiss have not shown much tolerance for cults, which are typically secretive and extreme in their beliefs. Eu-Wong explains that this intolerance began after members of one cult, believing the world would soon end, took their own lives:

> Cults have recently caused a furore [furor] in a small town called Cheiry near Geneva. Doomsday cults like the one started by Luc Jouret, a Quebecois [person from Quebec, Canada] doctor of questionable repute, had left a string of unsolved suicides [there] in the wake of his resettling in Switzerland. After 40 people had been lured into taking their own lives and the lives of their children [in the mid-1990s], many Swiss are more wary of quack religions.[17]

EDUCATION

Another aspect of Swiss life that varies dramatically according to region is education. Each canton establishes its own educational system, with no federal coordination of its activities. Therefore, the type of instruction used, the number of school days per year, the beginning and ending dates of the school year, the requirements for graduation, and many other aspects of education differ from one canton to the next.

There are certain generalities, however, that can be made about Swiss schools. They usually have very strict attendance requirements, and they often refuse to honor a parent's request that a child be allowed to leave early on a particular school day. Truancy is dealt with swiftly and severely. As a result, Swiss schools have some of the lowest absentee rates in the world. They also have longer hours than other European schools. In some cantons, students are required to attend school forty hours per week. School years, too, last on average far longer than elsewhere in Europe. Grades are handed out twice a year. There are four possible grades to receive, with a grade of 1 being the highest and 4 being the lowest.

About 95 percent of all Swiss students attend a public school run by a canton or community. About four hundred private schools also operate in Switzerland. Many of these are boarding schools. Private schools typically do not follow any Swiss models of education. Instead, most of them follow the curricula of British boarding schools, and a few are patterned after American ones. In either case, private schools are usually strict, somber, orderly, and fairly spartan.

In the Middle Ages, Swiss public schools were run by the Catholic Church, and only the children of nobles were educated. This began to change during the Restoration, when Protestants began promoting the idea of education for all. Then, in the 1840s, Switzerland started a public school system largely because of the efforts of Johann Heinrich Pestalozzi, a teacher who dedicated his life to helping the poor. He argued extensively that Swiss society as a whole would benefit from the education of poor children. As a result, any Swiss child can now attend public school for free, and the nearly 100 percent literacy rate can be attributed primarily to this policy.

While kindergarten attendance is optional in the country, 98 percent of parents choose to have their children attend this grade level. Attendance at primary and middle school—the latter of which is also called gymnasium—is mandatory. A student begins primary school at age six or seven, and attendance there continues for four to six years, depending on the canton. This means that in some cantons, a student entering middle school is only ten years old, whereas in others the student is thirteen years old. The number of years a student spends in

This statue depicts teacher Johann Heinrich Pestalozzi, who dedicated his life to helping Switzerland's poor.

middle school also varies. In many cantons the length of time is eight years, but in some, nine years are mandatory.

However, not all children in a canton attend the same type of middle school. Some are placed in a vocational gymnasium, where they learn a craft such as carpentry, while others go to an academic gymnasium, where they prepare for later university attendance. Academic gymnasiums are not all the same, however. Some emphasize mathematics and science, others language and literature. In other words, by the time a child is thirteen, his or her future career choices have already been limited.

Students who attend vocational schools typically learn not only in classrooms but also at workplaces. Swiss companies cooperate with cantons in providing on-the-job training. After

Swiss universities, such as the University of Lausanne, are funded by the individual cantons and from federal subsidies.

graduation, many students are offered employment by the companies where they served their apprenticeships.

Students who attend an academic gymnasium spend much of their time studying for an exam called the *Maturité*. A person's score on this exam determines which university he or she will attend or whether that person will be permitted to attend a university at all. Someone who has failed to earn a *Maturité* certificate typically spends the next two to four years as an apprentice learning a trade, just as though they had gone directly to a vocational gymnasium.

Students who do earn a *Maturité* certificate can immediately enter a university, though not necessarily their first-choice institution. Eu-Wong, who has lived in Switzerland, explains:

> Over the years we befriended students from various universities, and one of the things we discovered was that the number of applicants far outnumber the places available in universities. Therefore entrance exams are cruelly difficult to pass and only a small percentage of students are accepted into the faculty of their choice.[18]

A university education usually lasts seven years, although a few students can complete it in five. Most students stay in the same university the entire time; transferring from one university to another is rare. Universities are located in major cities, with roughly half in the German-speaking part of Switzerland and half in the French-speaking part. Those in German-speaking regions include the University of Basel, the University of Bern, and the University of Zurich. Those in French-speaking regions include the University of Geneva, the University of Lausanne, and the University of Fribourg. The university with the largest attendance is the University of Zurich, with over twenty thousand students.

Swiss universities are funded by the cantons, with subsidies from the federal government. There is only one private university in the entire country, the Theological Faculty in the city of Lucerne. There are, however, several private vocational institutions in Switzerland. Most train workers for jobs in the hotel, restaurant, or tourism industries. The government also funds vocational schools related to fields in which the demand for workers exceeds supply. In addition, every canton provides adult education classes related to language study, hobbies, parenting skills, and other topics of interest in the community.

SOCIAL SERVICES

Every canton also provides citizens with free health care, funded by mandatory contributions from employers and employees. As of 1948, all employers and employees have also been required to pay for Old-Age and Survivors Insurance, which provides living expenses to men over age sixty-five, women over age sixty-two, widows, orphans, and the disabled. The price of the insurance as well as how much the recipient ultimately receives is based on how much a person has earned.

However, the resulting amount is never enough to support all of a person's needs after retirement. Consequently, since 1972 the Swiss have also invested in a mandatory Company Pension Plan, also funded by employers and employees. For most people, these two types of savings plans are enough. But poor people, who have not earned much in their lifetimes, must also rely on subsidies provided by the federal government.

Cantons also make sure that their citizens have insurance to cover their losses in case of fire or theft. Someone who moves into a new dwelling typically receives a letter from the canton asking for a detailed list of his or her property as well as the value of each item. This is so the government can set a price for insuring the items through private insurance companies. In all, most Swiss people devote 10 percent of their annual income to paying for various types of insurance.

Whether funded at the local or federal level, most social services are distributed at the local level via the communes. Each commune makes sure that the Swiss citizens under its jurisdiction receive the minimum social services to which they are entitled, including health and retirement benefits. However, wealthier communes provide additional services, such as community centers that offer classes on hobbies or skills.

HOUSING

As with social services, housing varies greatly from canton to canton. Building styles have been influenced by the culture of a region's original settlers as well as by available raw materials. In the Ticino area of Switzerland near the Italian Alps, for example, houses are made entirely of rough stone, even the roofs. In the

In Ticino, near the Italian Alps, houses are built entirely from rough stone.

valley of Engadine, which is part of the Graubünden canton, the traditional house is made of smooth stone, although some houses are made of wood and are covered with stucco, a hard plaster, and have scenes or patterned designs painted on them.

In the Bernerse Oberland, the mountainous region around the city of Bern, houses and barns are often built as one structure. Moreover, because of the heavy snow in this region, houses are built with low pitched roofs, wide eaves all around, and shingles held in place with stones. The walls of some of these houses, called chalets, are decorated with pastoral art. In contrast, in the valleys of the Valais canton, houses—which can be four or five stories high—are made of wood and rest on wooden stilts. This keeps rats and mice from entering the home. Valais villages are also made entirely of wood. Bern was once made of wood, but after it was largely destroyed by a fire in 1405, it was rebuilt in sandstone. Its appearance remains much the same today as it did during the sixteenth century.

By studying the layout of Swiss villages, historians can tell much about why they developed where they did. According to the Phaidon Culture Guide to Switzerland,

Many chalets, some of which are decorated with pastoral art, are located in the Bernese Oberland.

Even today the layout of a town can say a great deal about its origins. Buildings like to spread themselves around churches and monasteries which were there before the town, as in [the cities of] St. Gallen and Bishofszell. If a castle on a hill was the starting point, then the town will be at the foot of that hill, as in Burgdorf and Thun. In other places several originally more or less independent settlements have merged . . . together over the centuries to create today's modern city.[19]

Many of the Swiss cities established during the Middle Ages were walled and/or otherwise fortified. Some of these cities still retain some or all of their fortification features, but many towns removed them during the nineteenth century. By this time, the Swiss people no longer felt they needed such heavy defenses, and population growth had used up all of the land within the walls.

Over four hundred thousand people live in Zurich.

MAJOR CITIES

The four largest cities in Switzerland are Zurich, Basel, Geneva, and Bern. Of these, Zurich has the largest population, with over four hundred thousand people. Built around Lake Zurich and the Limat River, its surrounding countryside has become heavily populated in recent years. Erika Schumacher reports that near Zurich, "villages and small towns which have delightful old centres . . . are surrounded by scars left by the building boom and the city dwellers' rush to live in the countryside." Schumacher suggests that this has destroyed some of the Old World charm of these areas, saying, "A whole variety of housing estates and blocks of flats, marked by very forced attempts at originality, often make the outskirts of villages resemble nothing more than three dimensional architectural showcases."[20] The original city of Zurich began in ancient times as a Roman customs post. It joined the Swiss Confeder-

✚ GENEVA

World peace is good for Geneva's pocketbook. The city's international organizations, which include the Red Cross, the United Nations, the World Council of Churches, the YMCA, and the Boy Scouts, provide Geneva's residents with over twenty-one thousand jobs. There are civil servants and over thirty thousand diplomats from over one hundred countries in the city, and they collectively spend over 1.2 billion Swiss francs a year in Geneva alone. One organization, the European Laboratory for Particle Physics, has six thousand visiting scientists a year as well as three thousand full-time employees. In addition, large meetings bring more dollars into the community. For example, a 1985 summit meeting between U.S. president Ronald Reagan and USSR president Mikhail Gorbachev brought four thousand journalists as well as thousands of police officers, soldiers, security experts, diplomats, political advisers, and other personnel.

ation in 1351, and since then it has been home to many important intellectuals as well as financial institutions. The people of Zurich are extremely hardworking and punctual, traits that some historians believe were instilled into the town's character when the strict preacher Huldrych Zwingli essentially ruled the city.

Basel is the second-largest city in Switzerland, with roughly 190,000 inhabitants. It is often called "the pharmacy of the world"[21] because it houses major chemical companies like Hoffman La Roche. The city is built along part of the Rhine River and lies on the border at the meeting point of Switzerland, France, and Germany. A major point of entry for goods, it has a river port, ferry boats, several bridges and railway stations, and a binational airport. These features have greatly affected its citizens' attitudes. Schumacher explains:

> [Basel] is like an island, whose inhabitants, despite being exposed to three different countries, are not noted for their openness: they are much happier keeping to themselves.... [Moreover] despite, or perhaps simply because of, the frontiers, the opportunity to escape and leave everything behind has always been an option that was readily available.[22]

Geneva is the third-largest city in Switzerland, with a population of around 180,000. Home to over two hundred international organizations, its residents are deeply involved in global

The bear, depicted atop this statue in Bern, is the city's emblem.

politics. In writing about the city, Schumacher says, "Nowhere else in Switzerland are arguments indulged in so eagerly, and words bandied about so assiduously as . . . in Geneva; nowhere else is there so much political discussion."[23] According to the German magazine *Stern*, Geneva also has the largest number of millionaires in Switzerland. Situated beside Lake Geneva, the largest freshwater reservoir in Europe, many of its businesses are involved in the manufacture of chemicals as well as timepieces and other precision instruments. Like Zurich, it also has many financial institutions.

The fourth-largest Swiss city is also the federal capital of Switzerland: Bern. Its population is roughly 150,000 people, many of whom work in the pharmaceutical or chocolate industries. Bern was built in 1191 by a duke, and today his original medieval city—situated on a ridge above the majority of Bern—is a popular tourist attraction with several museums. The city retains an aristocratic character, although it is not as bustling or as cosmopolitan as Switzerland's other large cities. It also has an element of quaintness: It is famous for its bears, which are the emblem of the city as well as of the Bern canton. Many buildings and squares in Bern have statues and/or paintings of bears, and an attraction known as the Bear Pit houses live bears. The name *Bern* means "bear" in Dutch; according to legend, the city was christened when Duke Berchtold V, upon selecting the town's location, decided to name it after the next animal he killed in a hunt.

Each of the four largest cantons has a different temperament. As with each canton, no two are alike. With such diversity, it has been difficult for the Swiss to maintain unity. Nonetheless, they have succeeded, largely because they do have a common culture. Leisure activities, in particular, have served to bind people of diverse cantons together. To be Swiss is to share certain interests, regardless of where one lives.

5

SWISS CULTURE

Despite their diversity, the Swiss people do have common cultural interests. They particularly enjoy sports, but they also take part in traditional activities like folk dancing. They share certain tastes in food as well as in art, music, and literature. These interests transcend differences created by canton-to-canton variations in language, religion, education, and other aspects of social life.

COMPETITIVE SPORTS

If the Swiss are passionate about anything, it is sports. They enjoy watching sports, whether in person or on television, but even more they enjoy participating in sports activities themselves. The reason for this is their environment, which is rich with opportunities for outdoor activities. As Shirley Eu-Wong notes,

> The Swiss are blessed with a country where the terrain provides ample opportunity for sports to be part and parcel of The Good Life. . . . The climate is suited seasonally to a variety of activities and to be bored by the countless sporting events can only mean one is deadly dull beyond redemption.[24]

Three popular sports, *Schwingen, Unspunnen Stein,* and *Hornussen,* are played only in Switzerland. *Schwingen* is a version of wrestling performed in a sand pit. It requires one of two opponents to be the first to lift and throw the other. *Unspunnen Stein,* also called stone-putting, is similar to shot-putting, with contestants heaving a stone as far as they can. (The city of Unspunnen is the place where the first stone-putting festival was held in 1805; the word *stein* means "stone.") *Hornussen,* called farmer's tennis, is played primarily in fields in the countryside around Bern. Actually it is more similar to baseball than to tennis. The game requires one player to hit a *hornuss,* or wooden disk, with a bat while other players some distance away try to catch it in a wooden racquet that has a net rather than the taut strings of a tennis racquet.

These sports, however, do not attract nearly as much interest as soccer, softball, or rifle shooting. Soccer is called football or *Fussball* in Switzerland, but it is played just as soccer elsewhere in the world. Softball is called *Schlagball* and uses four bases instead of three and a home plate. In this game, the ball is not pitched to the batter; instead, the batter tosses the ball up in the air and then hits it. Although both of these games are popular, more Swiss men are involved in shooting than in any other sport, and the Swiss Rifle Association is the largest sports organization in the country. This is largely because the Swiss must remain competent in shooting to meet their military service requirements.

Another powerful sports organization is the Federal Society of Gymnastics. To the Swiss, gymnastics means any type of organized physical exercise. People are encouraged to start participating in an activity while quite young, and they usually

Although the Swiss game of Hornussen *is called farmer's tennis, it bears a closer resemblance to baseball.*

continue to exercise regularly until quite old. In addition, the society sponsors gymnastics competitions that follow the same rules as gymnastic events in the Summer Olympics.

The Swiss have had many successes in the Summer Olympics, most notably in equestrian, or horseback-riding, events. Equestrian events include jumping and dressage, the latter of which requires the horse and rider to work together to perform a series of complicated movements. The Swiss have won many medals in equestrian events as well as in a variety of events held at the Winter Olympics. These include ice skating, bobsledding, skiing, and tobogganing.

WINTER SPORTS

In fact, the Swiss introduced the sport of tobogganing at the 1928 Winter Olympic Games, which they hosted. Tobogganing was invented in Switzerland to stave off winter boredom for nineteenth-century sanatorium patients. Like sleds, tobog-

Tobogganing was invented by the Swiss to entertain nineteenth-century sanatorium patients during the winter.

✚ TOBOGGANING

One of the first tobogganers was British author John Addington Symonds. While in Switzerland to improve his health, he tried out the sport and became perhaps the first person to write about it. According to travel writer Erika Schumacher in the guidebook *Switzerland,*

> An entry in Symonds's diary is one of the earliest references to how the sport started. After a dinner which lasted until two in the morning, complete with a zither and guitar player, he and two friends "descended on one toboggan in a dense snow-storm. It was quite dark and drifty beyond description." They got down all right, the diary notes, but not so "Miss I" who was on another toboggan. She completely lost control, flew over a photographer's hut and landed "on the back of her head on the frozen post-road. I fully expected to find her dead. She was only stunned, however."

gans were used for racing down snowy hills. The first toboggans were wooden boards with metal strips underneath, very different from today's sleek manufactured capsules.

Many children learn to toboggan or snowboard, but even more learn to ski. Both downhill and cross-country skiing, also called *Langlaufing,* are popular. Children start on the ski slopes very young, and although the Swiss primarily enjoy the sport in the winter, it is possible to ski in Switzerland year-round. This is because glacial mountain peaks in the Alps have snow even in the warmer months. To get to the best slopes, downhill skiers and snowboarders can use cable railways, chair lifts, or ski lifts. Beginners can learn to ski from one of over four thousand ski instructors in Switzerland, which has over two hundred ski schools and two hundred ski resorts. Most ski classes deal with downhill or cross-country skiing, but a few teach *Skikjöring,* which involves skiing across a frozen lake or flat slope while being pulled by a horse or vehicle.

Other popular winter activities in Switzerland are curling, ice skating, and ice hockey, which take place either on an ice-skating rink or on a frozen lake. Switzerland boasts more than eighty man-made ice-skating rinks and over fifteen hundred lakes, most of which freeze in the winter. Ice skating and ice hockey

Curling is a popular winter activity in Switzerland.

are well-known sports worldwide, but curling is popular primarily in western Europe. It requires teams of players to slide a special forty-pound granite stone toward a target. In doing this, some players use a broom to propel the stone while others throw it much like a bowling ball.

SUMMER SPORTS

Lakes are the site of many summer sports as well. These include sailing, water skiing, windsurfing, swimming, rowing, and yacht racing. Lake Geneva hosts the annual Bol d'Or, or Gold Cup, a sailing race that attracts many top competitors. Lake Sils is the location of the World Surfing Championships every July. Switzerland's rivers are the site of rafting and canoeing activities. The country also has more than 350 beaches, but most of them are private, meaning people must pay a fee to use them.

In contrast, the more than 31,068 miles of designated, well-marked hiking trails in Switzerland are free to use. Most of them have refreshment stands at regular intervals along the paths. Trails with easy terrain are called *Wanderweg*, and trails in the mountains are called *Bergweg*. There is also a unique hiking trail called the Mont Blanc Circuit, which winds its way through the Alps. The route is well marked, with entry points in three countries: France, Italy, and Switzerland. Completing the full circuit usually takes ten to fourteen days, with the hiker traveling 134 miles. The formalities involved with crossing a country border are waived along the route; in fact, there are no border markings at all. There are, however, way stations along the route where hikers can spend the night, although many people choose either to camp outdoors or to stay in nearby village hotels.

Many hikers also participate in mountaineering, or mountain climbing. There are many clubs and organizations devoted to this activity, as well as numerous mountaineering schools. During the 1950s the country sponsored one of the first mountaineering expeditions on the south side of Mount Everest in Nepal, and, although the team failed to reach the peak, it performed admirably.

Switzerland has more than 31,068 miles of designated, well-marked hiking trails.

Another popular Swiss sport is bicycling, which is also a form of transportation for many people. Trains allow passengers to bring bicycles on board, and most recreation areas rent bicycles. In the summer, cross-country bicycle races occur throughout the country. The most famous Swiss competition is the Tour de Suisse, a nine-day race held in June. The distance of the race is 1,000 miles, and each day the participants bike anywhere from 15 miles in the mountains to 150 miles in the flatlands.

HOLIDAYS AND FESTIVALS

Along with sports, the Swiss share an enjoyment of celebration. Many holidays and festivals are celebrated, most of which vary from canton to canton. A few, however, are common to all Swiss people. The most important of these are Swiss National Day, Christmas, and Easter.

Swiss National Day is observed annually on August 1 to commemorate the formation of the Swiss Confederation in 1291. On this date, the country celebrates with parades, fireworks, and parties that often include folk dancing and speeches. In some places, bells are rung and beacons lit; the latter is an ancient custom that developed when signal fires were used as a means of communication between one mountain town and another.

Christmas celebrations officially begin on December 6, which is also called Samiklaus Abend, or "Santa Claus Night." In many villages, someone dressed as Santa Claus goes from house to house to deliver candies and nuts to good children or a light spank with a willow switch to bad ones. Each child then tells Santa what he or she wants for Christmas, and Santa in turn passes this information along to the *Christikindli*, or Christ Child, who delivers the gift on Christmas Eve, December 24. The *Christikindli* is personified by a townsperson who goes to each house in a reindeer-drawn sleigh passing out gifts. The Swiss also have a custom of decorating a Christmas tree on Christmas Eve. Children do not participate in the decorating; instead, their parents make them leave the room before the tree is decorated and then surprise them with the finished result.

Easter is celebrated in Switzerland much as it is in the United States. People of all ages attend worship services in churches decorated with flowers and green branches. Children participate in Easter egg hunts and eat chocolate Easter bunnies. Can-

dlelit processions occur in some places on the seventh Sunday after Easter, which is called the Pfingsten, or "Feast of the Pentecost."

Other festivals occur throughout Switzerland at the beginning of Lent, which is a forty-day period of fasting prior to Easter Sunday. For instance, people in the city of Basel celebrate the Fastnacht, or "Fast Night," Carnival, which begins with a noisy parade through the streets at 4:30 in the morning. During the day there is much eating and celebrating. At night there is another parade, followed by a masked ball. Another celebration to mark the beginning of Lent occurs in the city of Flums, where men parade in wooden masks. In the city of Einsiedeln, men run through the streets rather than walk, while wearing not only masks but also heavy, clanging bells.

Zurich holds a parade during a two-day festival called the Sechseläuten, or "Six O'Clock Ringing," which commemorates a rebellion of workers against oppressive nobles. Held during either the second or third week of April, the festival concludes with the burning of a cotton figure, the *Böögg* (bogeyman), that has been doused with gasoline.

The Fastnacht Carnival begins at 4:30 in the morning with a parade through the streets of Basel.

FOOD

Although chocolate is a common food at many Swiss celebrations as well as in everyday life, the Swiss also enjoy a wide variety of cookies, pastries, and breads. One of their favorite cookies is the *Kräbeli*, which is flavored with aniseed. Another favorite, *Leckerli*, is a sweet biscuit filled with candied fruit and nuts. *Tirggel* is a cookie made of flour and honey and baked in a mold so that it comes out in the shapes of storybook figures or animals. *Ringli* is a cake baked in the shape of a wreath. Both cakes and tortes are extremely popular, and in the afternoon many people traditionally visit a bakery to enjoy one of these items with coffee as a snack. Bread with jam is another common snack. One traditional Swiss bread is *Eierzopf*, which is an eggbread whose dough has been braided into a loaf before baking. *Eierzopf* is typically eaten as part of breakfast.

Another breakfast food is *Müsli*, a mixture of oatmeal, fruit, nuts, and/or wheat germ mixed with either milk, yogurt, or both. It was invented in Switzerland at the end of the nineteenth century by Dr. Bircher-Brenner, who ran a health clinic. However, while *Müsli* is now popular in many parts of Europe and America, travel writer Mark Honan reports that it is not eaten much in Switzerland anymore:

> Go into any supermarket in Italy and half the shelves will be taken up with a thousand different varieties of pasta [a traditional Italian food]. In Swiss supermarkets you find maybe a couple of müsli packets tucked away in the corner and that's it. You're hardly force-fed the stuff as a visitor—it usually appears at lavish breakfast-buffets in the higher-class hotels, but the basic hotel breakfast is rolls, cheese, meat and jam, and that reflects national eating patterns.[25]

The main meal of the day typically includes meat, vegetables, and perhaps some form of cheese. According to Honan, the most common meats eaten in Switzerland are sausage, or wurst; veal, or *Kalbsfleisch;* and *Bündnerfleisch*, which is smoked, dried beef. Lake trout and perch are also popular. One of the most common vegetable dishes is *Rösti*, which consists of shredded fried potatoes similar to hash browns. A common cheese dish is *Raclette*, which is made with melted cheese and served with potatoes and baby onions. Fondue is a dish made with melted cheeses and white wine. Served in a pot, it is eaten by dipping bread cubes into the hot, liquidy mixture. Honan reports that when fondue is served at parties or in restaurants, "according to tradition, if your [bread] cube leaps off your fork and disappears in the [fondue] pot, you have to buy a round of drinks."[26] German, French, and Italian cuisine are often substituted for traditional Swiss fare, and Italian spaghetti and meatballs is a standard lunchtime meal in many places.

Main meals are eaten at noon, but a dish like *Omeletten*, which is egg pancakes served with fresh fruit or jam, is usually served later as a light supper. Also popular at supper are soups, which are typically very filling and often include dumplings called *Knöpfli*. As for beverages, adults often drink wine or beer; children drink fruit juice or apple cider served at room temperature. Milk is primarily used as an ingredient in cooking and baking rather than as a beverage. Favorite hot drinks are coffee, tea, and hot chocolate.

Fondue, a dish made with melted cheeses and white wine, is served in a pot and eaten by dipping bread cubes into the mixture.

FOLK ACTIVITIES

In addition to traditional foods, Swiss festivals often include folk music and dancing. The most traditional Swiss folk music is yodeling, which is a type of singing whereby the performer rapidly switches into and out of a falsetto voice to create a trilling effect. Other folk music relies not on the voice but on a musical instrument like the alpenhorn. Although similar to a trumpet, this instrument is made of wood and bark rather than brass. Traditional folk dances vary according to region, but one of the most popular is the *Schuhplatter*, which involves quick jumping and hopping movements.

People who participate in folk dancing often wear traditional costumes. Their style depends on region. For example, in the Gruyère region of the Fribourg canton, the traditional dress for men is a *Bredzon*, a short blue jacket with short puffy sleeves and embroidered lapels. For women, it is a long-sleeved jacket worn over a silk apron and simple dress. In contrast, in the for-

Some Swiss folk music uses an alpenhorn, an instrument made of wood and bark.

✚ Cows

Cows are an important part of Swiss life and often become the focus of many leisure activities. Many Swiss painters feature cow-herding scenes in their work, and woodworkers often make feed and water buckets for their cows, personalized with each animal's name. People in the region of Valais also enjoy attending cow fights, called the *Combat de Reines* in French and the *Kuhkämpfe* in German. In these battles, two combatants are placed in a ring and are encouraged to attack each other. The contest ends when one is fatigued but before either gets seriously hurt. The winner has traditionally been designated the leader of all herds in the area. In recent years, however, scientists have used advanced reproductive technology to cull embryos from the winner and implant them in "ordinary" cows for gestation. In this way, the cow's strength is passed on to as many offspring as possible.

mer canton of Unterwalden (which has since been divided into two cantons), women wear elaborately ornamented dresses and men wear elaborately embroidered shirts.

Embroidery is a popular folk hobby for women throughout the country. It adorns not only jackets, shirts, and dresses but also caps, scarves, and linens. They also spin yarn, knit, and weave, perhaps selling their crafts in *Heimatwerk*, or "homework," stores located in major cities. Meanwhile, many men are involved in woodcarving, chipping off curls and small pieces of wood that are used to decorate objects like milking stools. They also carve spoons, walking sticks, statues, and small figures. Folk museums display these objects as well as folk paintings in the *Sennenstriefen* style. These paintings, which typically portray cattle in farm or pasture settings, are made of paper or wood. *Senntum-Tafelbilder* are similar but smaller paintings done in watercolors on cardboard.

ARTISTS, MUSICIANS, AND WRITERS

Folk art is not particularly influential in the art world outside of Switzerland, but a Swiss art movement called Dada or Dadaism did have a great impact internationally. The word *dada* means "rocking horse" in French, and the name was supposedly chosen at random by the first Dada artists, a group of friends that included Hans "Jean" Arp, Richard Hülsenbeck,

Swiss Surrealist Alberto Giacometti works on one of his sculptures.

and Emmy Hennings. These artists developed the concept of Dadaism in 1916 while at a Zurich café called Hugo Ball's Cabaret Voltaire. It broke all of the established rules and customs of art at that time by presenting ordinary man-made objects as abstract art. The movement lasted only a short while, but most art historians believe it was the inspiration for a more lasting abstract movement, Surrealism, which occurred during the 1930s.

The most notable Swiss Surrealist is Alberto Giacometti, who worked during the 1930s through 1950s on such sculptures as *Head of Man on a Rod* and *Suspended Ball.* Other notable Swiss artists include landscape painter Ferdinand Hodler and abstract painter Paul Klee. Klee is perhaps the most famous of all Swiss artists, and art historians generally consider him one of the most influential artists of the twentieth century. Born in Bern in 1879, Klee attended art schools in Munich, Germany, from 1898 to 1901, and then traveled through Italy to study Renaissance paintings and through France to study French Impressionist art. Throughout his life, Klee continued to study fine art as he experimented with new and unusual styles and techniques to produce etchings, pen-and-ink and pastel drawings, and watercolor and oil paintings. His works include the etching *Der Held mit dem Flügel (Hero with the Wing)*, the pastel drawing *Figure im Garten (Figure in Garden)*, and the painting *Tod und Feuer (Death and Fire).*

In addition to artists, Switzerland has produced many fine musicians and writers. One of the greatest twentieth-century Swiss composers was Ernest Bloch. Although he was born in Geneva, he spent much of his life in the United States. One of his most famous symphonies was *Helvetia*, which honors Switzerland.

Two notable Swiss fiction authors are Johann David Wyss, who wrote *Swiss Family Robinson* in 1813, and Johanna Spyri, who wrote *Heidi* in 1881. Some of the most famous Swiss authors have been primarily identified as being philosophers. Of these, the most famous is Jean-Jacques Rousseau, who was born in Geneva in 1712. Rousseau's writings argued against monarchies and inspired revolutionaries in France to overthrow their rulers. Consequently, the Swiss government decided that Rousseau's ideas were too dangerous and expelled him from the country. Two other notable Swiss intellectuals were Jean Piaget and Carl Gustav Jung, early twentieth-century experts in human behavior. Psychologist Piaget concentrated on child development, identifying stages of physical and psychological growth that are still considered valid today. Psychiatrist Jung developed theories regarding personality and sexuality that helped form the basis of the field of modern psychology.

This statue depicts the famous Swiss philosopher Jean-Jacques Rousseau, who was expelled from Switzerland because of his "dangerous" ideas.

MYTHS AND LEGENDS

In addition to works written by specific authors, Switzerland has produced many myths and legends that have been passed down orally from one generation to the next. The most famous is the legend of William Tell, a thirteenth-century archer who refuses to kneel to show respect to a tyrant, a Habsburg named Gessler. As punishment, Gessler orders Tell to shoot an apple off the head of Tell's young son. If Tell misses, he will be executed and his son will probably be dead. Afraid to disobey for fear his son will be killed by the tyrant, Tell takes two arrows from his quiver, puts one arrow in his belt, and lets the other arrow fly. It hits the apple right in the middle, splitting it in half. When Gessler asks Tell what the second arrow is for, the archer explains that if he had accidentally killed his son, the arrow would have been used to shoot Gessler in the heart. An angry Gessler then imprisons Tell, but Tell soon escapes, tracks down Gessler, and does indeed shoot him in the heart. It is

said that Tell's actions inspired other Swiss people to rise up against Habsburg tyrants.

William Tell is a symbol of Swiss freedom and independence, a hero to the Swiss people. Historians disagree, however, on whether he was a real person. The theme of a good person rising up to conquer an evil one is common in Swiss myths. Sometimes the evil figure is the devil, but more often it is a tyrant like Gessler. Such stories reflect many qualities that are valued by the Swiss people. The hero stands up to unfairness courageously and honorably, often against great odds. But he typically succeeds not because of luck but because of skill and/or wit. He is clearly superior to his opponent, even though his opponent wields more power. Therefore, it is possible that the Tell story was a fictional one.

In modern times the Swiss strive to live their lives as honorably as their heroes. In general, they condemn dishonesty, work diligently at their jobs, strive to better themselves, promote healthy activities, and shun activities they believe to be physically or spiritually corrupting, such as gambling. Despite their country's difficult, divisive past and a geography that placed them in the midst of warring neighbors, they found ways not only to survive but to thrive. As reporter Rupert Cornwall once said of modern Switzerland,

> For the Swiss, theirs has been the land apart, which thanks to its valour, industry and good sense had avoided the traumas that engulfed the rest of Europe. It has seen itself as the purest distillation of independence and neutrality. . . . Depression, world wars, cold wars, the birth of a new Europe—come what may, Switzerland sailed serenely onward, rich and contented.[27]

FACTS ABOUT SWITZERLAND

GOVERNMENT

Form of government: Democratic; two-chamber legislature, with the Federal Assembly and the Federal Council. The Federal Assembly is made up of the National Council, which represents the people, and the Council of States, which represents the 26 cantons. The National Council has 200 seats with at least one representative elected from each canton; the Council of States has 46 members with two representatives elected from each canton. The Federal Council, or Cabinet, is the executive power, with seven members (each from a different canton) elected to four-year terms by the Federal Assembly and the Federal Council. The country's president is selected by the Federal Council.

Capital: Bern

Flag: White cross on a red background

LAND

Land area: 15,935 square miles

Length of the border: 1,170 miles

Highest mountains: Monte Rosa (15,203 feet), Dom (14,913 feet), Weisshorn (14,783 feet), Matterhorn (14,691 feet), and Dent Blanche (14,295 feet)

Longest glaciers: Aletsch Glacier (15 miles) and Gorner Glacier (9 miles), both in Valais canton

Largest lakes: Geneva (224 square miles), Constance (208 square miles), Neuchâtel (84 square miles), Maggiore (81 square miles), Lucerne (44 square miles), and Zurich (34 square miles)

Number of mountain railways: Approximately 500

PEOPLE

Population: 7,262,372, with 19.5% foreigners

Birth rate: 10.4 per 1,000

Death rate: 11.2 per 1,000

Infant mortality rate: 4.5 per 1,000

Life expectancy: 76.7 years male; 82.6 years female

Population growth rate: .3%

Ethnicity: German, 65%; French, 18%; Italian, 10%; Romansch, 1%; other, 6%

Literacy rate: 99% (1980 estimate)

Religious affiliations: Roman Catholic 46.1%; Protestant 40%; other 5%; none 8.9%

NATIONAL HOLIDAYS

(Days marked with an asterisk are religious holidays.)

January 1: New Year's Day

April: Good Friday*

April: Lundi de Pâcques* (Easter Monday)

May: Corpus Christi* (only celebrated in Roman Catholic cantons)

May 1: Labor Day (not celebrated in all cantons)

June 5: Ascension or Pentecostal Monday*

June 18: Fête-Dieu* (not celebrated in all cantons)

August 1: Swiss National Day

August 15: Assumption Day* (not celebrated in all cantons)

November 1: Touissaint* (not celebrated in all cantons)

December 6: St. Nicholas's Day* (not celebrated in all cantons)

December 8: The Immaculate Conception* (only celebrated in Roman Catholic cantons)

December 25: Christmas Day*

ECONOMY

Total number of workers (1990 estimate): 3,570,000; 900,000 of whom are foreigners

Labor breakdown: approximately 6% work in agriculture and forestry, 30% in industry, and 64% in the service sector

Average work week (1996 estimate): 43 hours

Monetary unit: Swiss franc, also called the CHF. Each franc can be divided into 100 centimes, also called rappen. Coins come in values of 5 centimes, 10 centimes, 20 centimes, 50 centimes, 1 franc, 2 francs, and 5 francs. Paper banknotes in denominations of 10, 20, 50, 100, 500, and 1000 francs, colored in orange, blue, and green.

Unemployment rate: 2.8%

NOTES

INTRODUCTION: A WEALTHY AND PRODUCTIVE NATION

1. Quoted in Mark Honan, *Switzerland: A Lonely Planet Travel Survival Kit.* Hawthorne, Victoria, Australia: Lonely Planet Publications, 1997, p. 25.

2. Honan, *Switzerland*, pp. 11–12.

3. Quoted in Honan, *Switzerland*, p. 13.

CHAPTER 1: A DIVIDED LAND

4. Quoted in Erika Schumacher, *Switzerland.* Singapore: APA Publications, 2000, p. 41.

CHAPTER 2: FROM A WARRING PEOPLE TO A UNIFIED NATION

5. Honan, *Switzerland*, p. 19.

CHAPTER 3: LAND OF PEACE AND PROSPERITY

6. Schumacher, *Switzerland*, p. 71.

7. Honan, *Switzerland*, p. 25.

8. Honan, *Switzerland*, p. 25.

9. Quoted in Schumacher, *Switzerland*, p. 72.

10. Quoted in Schumacher, *Switzerland*, p. 97.

11. Schumacher, *Switzerland*, p. 97.

12. Quoted in Schumacher, *Switzerland*, p. 75.

13. Schumacher, *Switzerland*, p. 89.

14. Shirley Eu-Wong, *Culture Shock! Switzerland.* Portland, OR: Graphic Arts Center, 1996, p. 26–27.

CHAPTER 4: MODERN SWISS PEOPLE

15. Eu-Wong, *Culture Shock!*, pp. 18–19.

16. Eu-Wong, *Culture Shock!*, p. 20.

17. Eu-Wong, *Culture Shock!*, pp. 30–31.

18. Eu-Wong, *Culture Shock!*, p. 84.

19. Phaidon Culture Guide, *Switzerland.* Englewood Cliffs, NJ: Prentice Hall, 1985, pp. 23–24.

20. Schumacher, *Switzerland*, p. 159.

21. Schumacher, *Switzerland*, p. 118.

22. Schumacher, *Switzerland*, pp. 116–17.

23. Schumacher, *Switzerland*, p. 303.

CHAPTER 5: SWISS CULTURE

24. Eu-Wong, *Culture Shock!*, pp. 68–69.

25. Honan, *Switzerland*, p. 61.

26. Honan, *Switzerland*, p. 61.

27. Rupert Cornwall, "Pity the Rich Swiss—They Have to Accept Their Own Normalty," *Independent*, February 26, 1998, p. 19.

CHRONOLOGY

B.C.

1500
First permanent settlers arrive in Switzerland.

58
Helvetian territory becomes part of the Roman Empire.

A.D.

400
The Alemanni take over what is now northern Switzerland.

500s
The Franks take control of what is now Switzerland.

600s
The Alemanni fight off the Franks.

700s
The Franks regain control from the Alemanni.

1032
Switzerland is united under the Holy Roman Empire.

1200s
The Habsburgs rise to power.

1291
Forest Cantons form confederacy to fight the Habsburgs.

1394
Five-year peace treaty is signed between the Swiss Confederation and the Habsburgs.

1400s
Switzerland becomes a major supplier of mercenaries in foreign wars.

1415
Twenty-year peace treaty is signed between the Swiss Confederation and the Habsburgs.

1476–1477
The Swiss defeat Charles the Bold.

1517
Martin Luther proposes reforms in the Catholic Church.

1523
Huldrych Zwingli establishes his own Protestant religion in Zurich.

1536
John Calvin visits Geneva and decides to establish his own Protestant religion there.

1648
Switzerland is declared a free land at the end of the Thirty Years' War.

1798–1803
Napoléon takes over Switzerland for France; establishes Helvetic Republic.

1815
Congress of Vienna makes Switzerland an independent, neutral country.

1847
Swiss civil war occurs.

1848
New constitution is adopted.

1864
First Geneva Convention takes place; Swiss Alps become prime tourist destination.

1874
Swiss constitution is revised.

World Wars I and II
Switzerland remains neutral and accepts refugees.

1920s–1930s
The League of Nations meets in Geneva.

1971
Women are given the right to vote.

1979
The newest Swiss canton, Jura, is established.

1986
Swiss voters reject membership in the United Nations.

1992
The Swiss people vote against becoming a member of the
EEA (European Economic Area), a group of European coun-
tries dedicated to addressing common economic issues.

1995
Switzerland experiences its first high unemployment since
the global depression of the 1930s.

1997
Nazi Gold Scandal occurs.

SUGGESTIONS FOR FURTHER READING

David Birmingham, *Switzerland: A Village History.* New York: St. Martin's, 2000. This book focuses on life in the village of Château d'Oex in the Gruyère region of Switzerland.

Gerry Crawshaw, *Essential Switzerland.* Lincolnwood, IL: Passport Books, 1994. Crawshaw's guidebook offers many facts about Switzerland.

Hans Rathgeb, *Baedeker's Switzerland.* Englewood Cliffs, NJ: Prentice Hall, 1982. Rathgeb's guidebook provides facts and photographs for modern travelers to Switzerland.

Johanna Spyri, *Heidi.* New York: Aladdin Classics, 2000. This is a new edition of one of the classic works of Swiss literature about a girl who grows up on an Alpine mountain but later must adjust to life in a Swiss city.

WORKS CONSULTED

BOOKS

Joy Charnley and Malcolm Pender, eds., *Switzerland and War*. New York: Peter Lang, 1999. This book offers analyses of Swiss warfare and neutrality throughout history.

Rupert Cornwall, "Pity the Rich Swiss—They Have to Accept Their Own Normalty," *Independent*, February 26, 1998. This article discusses modern pressures on Switzerland, particularly in regard to its refusals to join the European Union.

Bob Edwards, "Profile: Increasing Popularity of Car-Sharing Plan in Switzerland," *Morning Edition*, National Public Radio, March 15, 2000. This radio program discusses a Swiss car-sharing system designed to help reduce air pollution.

Shirley Eu-Wong, *Culture Shock! Switzerland*. Portland, OR: Graphic Arts Center, 1996. Based on the experiences of a foreigner living in Switzerland, this guidebook offers tips on how to adjust to life in Switzerland.

David Hampshire, *Living and Working in Switzerland: A Survival Handbook*. Surrey, UK: Survival Books, 1991. Intended to help foreigners moving to Switzerland deal with everyday life there, this guidebook offers helpful information about Swiss culture.

Mark Honan, *Switzerland: A Lonely Planet Travel Survival Kit*. Hawthorne, Victoria, Australia: Lonely Planet Publications, 1997. This travel guidebook provides information not only about sight-seeing opportunities in Switzerland but also about Swiss history and culture.

Phaidon Culture Guide, *Switzerland*. Englewood Cliffs, NJ: Prentice Hall, 1985. This guidebook focuses on Swiss culture rather than history or sight-seeing opportunities.

Erika Schumacher, *Switzerland*. Singapore: APA Publications, 2000. This guidebook offers many excellent photographs of

Switzerland along with fairly detailed information about Swiss history, culture, and lifestyle.

WEBSITES

http: www.cia.gov/cia/publications/factbook/geos/sz.html. The Central Intelligence Agency World Factbook 2000 contains the most current facts about Switzerland.

INDEX

PICTURE CREDITS

ABOUT THE AUTHOR

Patricia D. Netzley received a bachelor's degree in English from the University of California at Los Angeles (UCLA). After graduation she worked as an editor at the UCLA Medical Center, where she produced hundreds of medical articles, speeches, and pamphlets.

Netzley became a freelance writer in 1986. She is the author of over two dozen books for children and adults, including *The Curse of King Tut* and *UFOs* for Lucent Books. She and her husband, Raymond, live in southern California with their children, Matthew, Sarah, and Jacob.